WEIRD PEOPLE

We Are Stranger Than We Think

JOCELYN LITTLE

STERLING PUBLISHING CO., INC.
NEW YORK

Library of Congress Cataloging-in-Publication Data

Little, Jocelyn.
    Weird people : we are stranger than we think / by Jocelyn Little.
      p. cm.
    Includes index.
    ISBN 0-8069-3850-1
    1. Parapsychology. I. Title.
  BF1031.L52   1966
  133—dc20   95-51256
                                                      CIP

10 9 8 7 6 5 4 3 2 1

Published by Sterling Publishing Company, Inc.
387 Park Avenue South, New York, N.Y. 10016
© 1996 by Jocelyn Little
Distributed in Canada by Sterling Publishing
c/o Canadian Manda Group, One Atlantic Avenue, Suite 105
Toronto, Ontario, Canada M6K 3E7
Distributed in Great Britain and Europe by Cassell PLC
Wellington House, 125 Strand, London WC2R 0BB, England
Distributed in Australia by Capricorn Link (Australia) Pty Ltd.
P.O. Box 6651, Baulkham Hills, Business Centre, NSW 2153, Australia
Manufactured in the United States of America

Sterling   ISBN 0-8069-3850-1

CONTENTS

PEOPLE WITH STRANGE POWERS

Some of our powers are commonplace, yet can seem quite remarkable when you think about them. How is it that you know someone is looking at you, even if you are facing away? The phone rings and you know who it is before you pick it up. How? Many people can fall asleep and wake up at the exact time they wish to. How do they do that? The point is, we all may have strange powers.

• • •

A psychic named Phoebe Payne had the ability as a little girl to see the auras of flowers. She was surprised to learn the pretty colors she saw were invisible to other people.

• • •

A boy in South Africa could see water deep underground "shimmering like green moonlight." He became known as "the boy with the X-ray eyes" for his strange ability. The boy was shocked when he was told that other people could not see as he did.

• • •

The psychic Ingo Swann first discovered his powers at the tender age of two. He underwent a tonsillectomy and watched the entire procedure in an out-of-body experience. The walls turned iridescent colors as he went under anaesthesia, and he floated above the operating table. Swann watched as a nurse took the tonsils and hid them in a glass jar on a shelf behind some rolls of paper. When he awoke, he demanded to be given the tonsils, and he astonished everyone when he knew where they were. Ingo Swann became an artist, painting the vivid colors of the auras he saw around people and animals.

• • •

The actress Helena Modjeska (1840–1909) is said to have reduced an entire dinner party to tears by her dramatic reading of a speech in Polish. Her audience did not understand a word she said, but were deeply moved anyway. It turned out she had simply recited the alphabet.

• • •

An Indian holy man named Sai Baba performs miracles, or so his followers say. He heals the sick; teleports himself; levitates; and produces gold, jewels, and flower petals from thin air. Once he caused a supply of food to multiply a hundredfold. It is even claimed he brought a dead man back to life. The man was named Radhakrishna; he was blue, stiff, lifeless, and starting to decompose when Sai Baba asked to be left alone with him. Radhakrishna walked out of the room full of life and cured of the ailment that had killed him. No one has yet been able to establish fraud or trickery in the powers of Sai Baba.

• • •

Dr. Wolfgang Larbig, of the University of Tübingen in Germany, hooked up an Indian yogi to medical equipment to find out what happened when he went into a trance. The yogi stabbed himself in the stomach and neck and tongue with metal spikes, yet showed no pain and did not bleed. His brain waves remained in a theta pattern, as if he were asleep and dreaming. The conductivity of his skin was abnormal, as if there were another barrier between him and the pain.

• • •

Jack Schwartz was untrained, but he had the same powers the Indian yogis and Tibetan monks acquired after years of study. Schwartz could stab himself without pain or blood, read minds, and heal with his hands. In the laboratory, he stuck a thick sailmaker's needle through his biceps. The experimenter asked him if he could make the wound bleed normally. Blood gushed for about 10 seconds; then Schwartz said softly, "Now it stops." Instantly the wound closed up as if drawn together with purse strings, and not another drop of blood appeared.

• • •

A 23-year-old Swedish woman known only as Maria K. was the victim of a severe beating. Long after the wounds healed, however, she continued to bleed sporadically from the ears, eyes, and scalp. Doctors found she could will herself to do so, if emotionally worked up.

• • •

Rosa Kuleshova grew up in a family of blind people. She is sighted but taught herself to see with her fingers. She can distinguish colors and read newspapers, books, or sheet music while completely blindfolded. An intervening pane of glass does not diminish her fingers' ability to see, and she can also see with her elbow.

The psychologist Novomeisky was one of a team of Soviet scientists who tested Kuleshova relentlessly in the 1960s. He continued his experiments on other people and found that ordinary people can distinguish the different textures of colors within a few hours. They agreed that yellow is slippery, red is sticky, and violet makes the fingers stop. They also said colors have different heights.

• • •

A young Japanese girl named Sayori Kanaka can see with her nose. Completely blindfolded, she can bike down a busy street, read a magazine, or catch balls thrown at her from 6 yards (5.4 metres) away.

• • •

In the late 19th century, an Italian neurologist named Cesare Lombroso described a 14-year-old blind girl who could read and see with her left earlobe and the tip of her nose. Once when Dr. Lombroso started to prod her nose with a pencil, the girl cried indignantly, "Are you trying to blind me?"

• • •

The Frenchman Etienne Bottineau was renowned in his day for his remarkable eyesight. He could "see" ships before they appeared on the horizon by interpreting the atmospheric disturbances they created. From the 1760s to the 1780s, he was beacon-keeper on the island of Mauritius. He did not use a telescope, yet he discerned ships 100 to 600 miles (160 to 960 km) away. Tested over a 6-month period, Bottineau correctly predicted the arrival of 109 ships before they docked. The two ships that did not arrive as he predicted were later determined to have changed course.

• • •

A nun from Detroit named Sister Barbara Burns had noted for years that her eyesight was failing. In July 1971 she decided to try a visualization technique called Silva Mind Control. She repeated to herself the phrase: "Every time I blink my eyes, they will focus accurately, like the lens of a camera." After two weeks she gave up wearing glasses except for reading. Some astigmatism remained, so she willed her corneas to correct their shape. A year after she started, Sister Barbara did not need glasses at all.

• • •

Peter Sugleris says he can levitate at will, though it is a tremendous strain and may take months to prepare. In February 1986, Sugleris's wife videotaped him rising from the kitchen floor to a height of 18 inches (45 cm), and remaining suspended in midair for 47 seconds. The grimace of concentration on his face was so fierce, Sugleris frightened his wife. She said he looked as if he would burst. He sweated profusely and nearly blacked out afterwards.

• • •

Sister Maria Coronel de Agreda was a 17th-century nun who lived in Spain but could appear at will anywhere in the world. By her own account she "bilocated"—or appeared in two places at once—over 500 times between 1620 and 1631. She also levitated on occasion, but struggled against it. She was horrified when she discovered that the other nuns had displayed her while she was in a trance.

Sister Maria appeared regularly to a poor Indian tribe called the Jumanos, who lived along the Rio Grande in what is now Presidio, Texas. The Jumanos called her their gentle ''lady in blue.'' She ministered to them and converted many to Christianity. When a Franciscan priest arrived in the normal way, he was dismayed to find most of the tribe had already been converted.

• • •

Saint Joseph of Cupertino was a simple man with a powerful devotion to God, which was expressed by his ability to levitate and even fly. He joined the Capuchin order in 1620, but his devotions were too extreme and he was dismissed. Saint Joseph then joined a monastery at Grottaglie, Italy, where he began levitating with regularity, once in the presence of Pope Urban VIII. While praying in a church in Naples, he shrieked in rapture and flew to the altar, landing among the burning candles and alarming the nuns. Saint Joseph cured a lunatic named Baldassare by seizing him by the hair and carrying him aloft for 15 minutes. On another occasion, he was walking in a garden with another priest, who mentioned something about the beauty of heaven. Saint Joseph shrieked and flew to the top of an olive tree and knelt on a slender branch. He was afraid of heights, so when he came out of his rapture the other priest had to get him down with a ladder.

• • •

A teacher who worked in Russia in 1845 had an amazing ability. One day in class, her students saw two images of her at the same time; one was teaching and the other was strolling around outside picking flowers. Another day they saw her simultaneously facing the class and writing on the blackboard. A friend sitting at the teacher's bedside when she was sick was startled to see her double walking around the room.

The teacher, known as Madame Sage, told her superiors she

had the power to project an image of herself at will. She was not surprised when she was dismissed.

• • •

Jacques Aymar was a Frenchman who lived in the late 17th century. He discovered his dowsing abilities at an early age. While dowsing for water at one place, he dug down and was horrified to discover the decapitated head of a woman. He later visited the dead woman's home and his divining rod pointed at her husband, identifying him as her killer. Aymar became a successful diviner of criminals.

• • •

Chiero the Great was the best known fortune-teller of his day. He arrived in New York City in 1893 from London. Reporters tested him by showing him the palm prints of 13 people. Chiero correctly described the identities of 12, including one of the actress Lillian Russell, whom he described as a child of fate with talent and ambition. He refused to identify the 13th palm print until he was challenged. "This is the mark of a murderer," he said dramatically. "He will give himself away through his own self-confidence and will die in prison." The handprint belonged to a Dr. Henry Meyer, who was in the Tombs prison, charged with murder. He was convicted and died insane, behind bars.

• • •

Beverly Jaegers of Missouri made a broker a millionaire in 1974 through her psychic gifts. She believes paranormal powers are not fleeting and unreliable, but can be used regularly and productively. The broker gave her an envelope, which contained questions about coffee futures, and she saw in a vision that there would be a poor coffee harvest. The broker invested accordingly; when the stocks paid off, he bought her a $60,000 house in gratitude. Stockholders all over the world then wrote to her for advice. Jaegers would handle each envelope, and if it "felt hot," she would tell them the stock was good. In 1982, the *St. Louis Business Journal* tracked Jaegers against 19 leading stockbrokers. The portfolios picked by 16 lost value. Her stocks increased over 17%, even though the entire market lost value during that time.

• • •

Wolf Messing was a Polish psychic who fled to Russia to escape the Nazis in World War II. He feared for his life because he was Jewish and because he had predicted Hitler's downfall if he invaded Russia. Messing attracted the attention of the dictator Josef Stalin, who tested him. Messing was challenged to make his way into Stalin's private office inside his heavily guarded compound in the country. He walked through the gates in broad daylight, past the guards who had been ordered to stop him, and into Stalin's office. The dictator was astonished and asked how it was done. Messing explained that he had convinced the guards telepathically that he was Beria, the feared head of the secret police, even though they looked nothing alike.

Messing had discovered this telepathic ability as a boy, when he hid from a train conductor under a seat because he did not have any money. The conductor hauled him out and demanded a ticket. In desperation, Messing gave him a scrap of newsprint and willed him to accept it. The conductor looked at the paper for a long minute, then stamped it and asked in a puzzled voice, "Why are you hiding under the seat when you have a ticket?"

• • •

Aleister Crowley was a thoroughly despicable individual who set up a cult called the Golden Dawn in Europe in the early 1900s. He left his baby to die of typhoid in India, for fear of catching the disease himself. Both his wives died insane. On an attempt to climb the third highest mountain in the Himalayas, his team was buried in an avalanche and Crowley made no attempt to rescue them. He would merit no mention in this book but for a strange incident in New York. Crowley and a friend were walking down Fifth Avenue. He said, "Watch this," and he followed a stranger, imitating his gait and keeping perfect step. Suddenly Crowley collapsed and fell sideways. The stranger also collapsed and fell in exactly the same way. True to form, he left the man in a crumpled heap and continued on his way unperturbed.

• • •

The anthropologist Taomas Roessner studied native tribesmen in a remote area of eastern Peru. They had no contact with modern conveniences or civilization, but the shaman received visions of faraway lands. Roessner was asked, "What are those strange things that run so swiftly along the street?" The tribesmen had seen automobiles in their psychic visions but could not understand what they were.

• • •

Explorer Laurens van der Post described the Bushmen of the Kalahari in his book *Lost World of the Kalahari.* He went hunting with the men of the clan, and they killed game about 50 miles from camp. One of the hunters told van der Post their women knew they had procured meat. When van der Post expressed amazement, the Bushman tapped his chest and said, "We bushpeople have a wire here that brings us news."

• • •

George McMullen specialized in psychometric readings of archeological artifacts. He caused a sensation at a meeting of the Canadian Archeological Association in 1973, when he identified a crudely carved black stone found in the Queen Charlotte Islands as having been done by a slave from West Africa. No black slaves were thought to be in the Maritimes of Canada at that time period. McMullen picked up psychically that the carver had been kidnapped to the Caribbean, then sold to an Englishman and taken on board a ship bound for California. The slave escaped and joined a group of Canadian Indians. A graduate student who did not know the stone's origin recognized it as resembling masks from Sierra Leone. Intriguing confirmation came much later when descendants of a group of Canadian Indians told of an African ancestor.

• • •

Stefan Ossowiecki was a psychic archeologist. He would hold an artifact in his hands, go into a trance, and describe the long-dead people and culture that produced it. Many of the details he described were later confirmed.

A Hungarian named Dionizy Jonky left a sealed package in his will to be used as a test of this ability. Ossowiecki identified Jonky's picture among 14 others, though they had never met. In front of 50 witnesses, Ossowiecki then handled the package. He said, "Volcanic minerals. There is something here that pulls me to other worlds, to another planet. It's part of a meteorite. There's also traces of sugar here." The package was opened. It contained pieces of a meteorite, wrapped in a candy bar wrapper.

Ossowiecki worked with fellow Pole Professor Stanislau Poniatowski in the 1930s. When Hitler invaded, the two men stayed and provided readings for worried relatives of missing soldiers and those that had been taken to extermination camps. The Gestapo arrested Poniatowski in 1942 and shot him just before the war ended. Ossowiecki had foretold, "I see that I will die a terrible death, but I have lived a wonderful life." In 1944, German soldiers machine-gunned nearly 10,000 Warsaw citizens in a public park. One of the massacred was Ossowiecki.

• • •

A distinguished surgeon, Dr. Gerald Feigen, described a firewalk on a dark and windy night in Bora Bora. The priest, Tanatos, arrived in dramatic fashion, with his helpers wearing grass skirts and carrying torches. Tanatos said, "Goddess of the Moon, favor us," and the clouds parted and the moon came out. Then he said, "Goddess of the Wind, favor us," and the wind stopped. The fire pit had been burning for three days, and the heat was intense. A young American couple walked across it, stamping their bare feet, and showed no signs of injury.

Dr. Feigen felt an overwhelming confidence that he could do the firewalk as well. So he took off his shoes and socks and went across. From the knees down his legs and feet felt cool. The intense feeling of confidence and calm carried him across the hot coals. He said later, "You don't need to have some kind of mysterious chemical that you rub on your feet, or go into any kind of training. All you have to do is believe and surrender."

• • •

When Jennie Morgan of Sedalia, Missouri, reached her early teens, she inexplicably began to give off charges of electricity. She shot sparks from her hands that sometimes knocked people unconscious. Her presence frightened animals away. Doctors were baffled and the girl felt she was cursed. The electricity went away when Morgan reached adulthood.

• • •

Angelique Cottin, a 14-year-old French girl who worked as a glovemaker in Normandy in 1846, had an episode of 10 weeks' length when everything she touched reacted violently. Compasses spun wildly, heavy furniture vibrated or moved away at her approach, the wooden frames she worked with twisted themselves, her bed rocked, and her slightest touch sent large objects flying.

• • •

Louis Hamburger was a human magnet. He could make heavy metal objects dangle from his fingers. He lifted a glass beaker filled with iron filings by just touching it. When one of his fingers was tugged away, it made an audible click.

• • •

Frank McKinstry of Joplin, Missouri, had to keep walking once he started down the street. If he paused, his feet would become rooted to the ground with a magnetic force so powerful that he would have to ask a passerby to free him.

• • •

In the late 1980s, a young woman named Inga Gaiduchenkova of Byelorussia showed a remarkable ability to magnetize objects by touching them. She also had some success treating patients with poor circulation by laying on hands.

• • •

A Polish teenager's ability to move objects without touching them was first noticed when light bulbs exploded when she entered a room.

• • •

In 1850 a Colonel Bethune bought a slave child named Blind Tom. Tom had been born blind and retarded but had an extraordinary ability. After hearing any piece of music once, he could play it again, flawlessly, on the piano. Blind Tom could neither read music, nor see the keys, nor explain his ability. He would even play mistakes other pianists made. He eventually learned over 5000 pieces of music and once performed for President James Buchanan. Colonel Bethune exploited the boy as a sideshow freak.

• • •

Alonzo Clemens only has an IQ of 40, but he creates sculptures of remarkable beauty. He works in clay and his animal sculptures are full of life. He captures not only the appearance of the animals, but the essence of them. He has never had art lessons and is what used to be called an "idiot savant."

• • •

Rabbi Elijah of Lithuania could read and retain every word of every book he read. He regarded this ability as a curse, as he was unable to forget any word of the 2000 books he read in his lifetime.

BIRTH

During the Civil War battle of Raymond in Mississippi, May 12, 1863, a young Union soldier was wounded. A bullet hit him in the groin and carried away his left testicle. The same bullet penetrated the wall of a nearby house and finally ended its flight in the lower abdomen of the 17-year-old girl who lived there. Nine months later, the girl, who was a virgin, gave birth to a baby boy. The attending physician who reported the bizarre case, Dr. T. G. Capers, operated on the baby and removed the remarkable bullet. He concluded that the girl had been impregnated by the sperm carried on the bullet. Dr. Capers introduced the two young people to each other and they eventually married. They had three more children, but the oldest boy resembled his father the closest.

• • •

A woman in West Germany gave birth in 1978 to twin baby boys, one white and one black. She had had intercourse with a white German and a black American on the same day and had ovulated twice. The twins were sent to separate foster homes.

• • •

A high school English teacher in Louisiana went into labor in October 1994, but did not know it and kept teaching. Her students recognized her symptoms as many were mothers themselves. She was carrying twins and the labor was premature, so doctors tried to delay delivery. A baby boy was born 4 days later, weighing only 1 pound 14 ounces. His twin sister was born three months later, weighing 6 pounds; her hospital bill was $850. The baby boy's hospital bill was $225,000.

• • •

A woman in San José, California, was born with two uteruses. She gave birth to twins. One twin was delivered by Caesarean from the left uterus; the other was a vaginal birth from the right uterus, eight days later.

• • •

Gladys Wright of Norfolk, England, was a country midwife. On a blustery December night in 1952, she found herself unable to either sleep or stop thinking about a particular patient. Finally she felt compelled to visit the woman, despite her husband's protests. She arrived at 2 o'clock in the morning and the house was all lit up. Her patient's husband was just leaving to fetch the midwife when she arrived. The pregnant woman was standing in her kitchen, very worried, and in labor. Mrs. Wright successfully delivered a healthy, though premature, baby boy.

• • •

Expectant mothers in Los Angeles are reporting remarkable results after eating the salad at the Caioti Café. They say eating the romaine and watercress salad, with oil and vinegar dressing, induces labor within a few hours. The owner, Ed LaDou, says the salad dressing, which contains balsamic vinegar, is responsible. He says 18 of his customers have started contractions within 5 hours of eating the salad. Balsamic vinegars are aged in wooden barrels, and a fungus that grows in those barrels can cause contractions of the uterus.

• • •

When anesthesia was introduced for use in childbirth in the 1840s, some clergymen objected, because the Bible says that women shall give birth in sorrow. Their objections were quashed when Queen Victoria used anesthesia while giving birth to her seventh child. The Queen was above reproach.

• • •

The offspring who is conceived when a couple is trying to make a baby tends to be of the same sex as the parent who feels the least stress at the time. A woman who feels pressure to produce a daughter is ironically more likely to give birth to a son, and a man who feels stressed to father a son is more likely to beget a daughter.

• • •

Men who drink heavily father girls more often. Alcohol decreases the testosterone needed to father boys.

• • •

Drinking lots of orange juice can keep a man's sperm healthy.

• • •

The *University of Pennsylvania Journal of Medicine* reported a case of a woman with 9 breasts, 5 of which produced milk.

• • •

In many cases, people other than childbearing women can produce milk in their breasts. Men, children, and postmenopausal women have produced milk. Spontaneous milk production sometimes occurs when problems with the pituitary gland cause the release of prolactin.

• • •

Embryos at various stages have gills, a tail, a two-chambered heart, and three pairs of kidneys—all leftovers from our ancestors. They evolve into more familiar body structures by the time the baby is born. But other leftovers remain. That fold of pink tissue in the corner of your eye is what is left of the nictitating membrane, the moist layer of skin that masks the eyes of amphibians and wipes the eyes of birds. And the groove in your upper lip was once a moist fleshy part of your nose, something like a dog's nose.

• • •

All fetuses spend the last few weeks in the womb covered with a soft coat of hair called the lanugo. It covers the whole body except for the palms of the hands and the soles of the feet. Sometimes a baby is born covered in the downy hair, but it will eventually fall out. The lanugo is a reminder that we are all descendants of hairy mammals.

• • •

Morning sickness is a condition very common in Western society. It is apparently not a universal symptom of pregnancy, however, and in less advanced societies it is all but unknown.

• • •

The most common position in which to give birth in traditional societies is sitting upright, with the knees pulled up to the chest, and the mother leaning on a support, or holding herself up. The second most common position is kneeling. The third is squatting, which is a more difficult one in which to keep balance. Hard as it is to believe, some women traditionally give birth *standing*.

• • •

An estimated 1,000 women died giving birth today.

BABY

Babies still in the womb sometimes get hiccups.

• • •

A 4-month-old fetus will startle and turn away if a bright light is flashed on its mother's belly.

• • •

Babies in the womb react to sudden loud noises, even if their mother's ears are muffled.

• • •

A newborn can distinguish the sound of his father's voice from that of another man. This is more likely to happen if the father talked to him in the womb.

• • •

A newborn only 15 minutes old can start to imitate the expression on its mother's face.

• • •

Fathers of newborn babies were able to correctly identify their infants simply by stroking the backs of their hands. Nearly two-thirds of the fathers were able to distinguish their own among three babies of similar age, sex, and size. The fathers were blindfolded and had their noses covered in the study, which was done in Jerusalem in the 1980s. Mothers of newborn babies could also pick out their own in the same way, and they could also distinguish their own infant by stroking their cheeks, which the fathers could not do.

• • •

A woman gave birth in a toilet on a moving train in Mozambique. She was washing the newborn when he slipped from her hands and fell into the toilet, then out onto the train tracks. At least four trains passed over the section of track before the baby was found, healthy and unharmed, several hours later. The mother was hospitalized for shock.

• • •

6-day-old babies can distinguish their mother's personal scent. The newborn will turn toward the smell of its mother and away from the scent of a stranger.

• • •

After only 3 nights, a mother will wake to the sound of her own newborn crying and will sleep through the crying of other infants.

• • •

Most human babies start smiling at the age of 4 weeks. It is widely assumed that babies smile in response to their parents' faces, but babies born blind start to smile at the same age.

. . .

Girl babies smile longer and more often than boy babies. They cry less and are quicker to potty train.

. . .

As a general rule, a child will speak its first three words by 12 months, 19 words by 15 months, 22 words at 18 months, and then an explosive jump to 118 words at 21 months and 272 words at 2 years of age. This is not purely a matter of learning, as toddlers are "programmed" to begin to talk, although neglect may slow down the process.

. . .

Young children enjoy it if you talk very fast to them. If you show children a machine that can regulate the speed of recorded speech, they choose to listen to about 175 words a minute. Blind children like it even faster—about 275 words a minute.

THE HUMAN BODY

The speed of thought is 150 miles (240 km) per hour.

• • •

The brain runs on the same amount of energy as would light a 10-watt bulb.

• • •

Your head weighs about 12 pounds (5.4 kg), or the same as a light bowling ball.

• • •

If we didn't get any niacin in our food, we would become insane in less than a year.

• • •

Stomach acid can dissolve razor blades.

• • •

Urine is sterile. It is cleaner than saliva until exposed to bacteria in the air.

• • •

Blood is blue. It turns red when exposed to oxygen.

• • •

Before you cut yourself, the skin anticipates and limits blood loss by shrinking blood vessels in the area. Take a flat ruler and scrape the edge along your arm. That white line you drew is caused by the shutoff of blood where pressure is felt. Once the danger is past, the brain signals the okay for blood to return to the area.

• • •

Bone is almost identical in content to some kinds of South Pacific coral. Some plastic surgeons are taking advantage of this by using coral to replace bones in the face. The body does not reject coral as it might a bone transplant.

• • •

There are so many preservatives in our food these days that our bodies don't decompose as fast as bodies used to.

• • •

North American Indians sometimes used to starve in late winter even if they caught plenty of game. The wild animals yielded very lean meat, and no matter how much they ate, the Indians could starve to death without some fat in their diet.

• • •

Traditional societies all around the world distinguish between simple hunger and craving for meat. Natives of Malaysia may stuff themselves with rice and vegetables but say, "I haven't eaten for days," if there is no meat in their diet. The Kaingang people regarded only meat as food, all else as garnish.

• • •

Drinking seawater does not cause insanity. Drinking nothing but seawater, however, will eventually cause your kidneys to fail and can kill you.

• • •

Because we are mostly water, and that water has the same salt content as seawater, we are affected by the tides. Every time the tide rises, we lose a fraction of an ounce in weight, only to gain it back again.

• • •

It is thought the Chinese accidentally discovered acupuncture during ritual bloodletting with pinpricks. Bloodletting evolved from more copious amounts to token drops, and Chinese priests found that pins stuck in different parts of the body relieved pain and cured ailments. Over the centuries, these observations became an established medical art. Acupuncturists can even relieve the ''phantom pain'' of amputees.

• • •

The latest artificial limbs include sensors that connect to nerves in the patient's body. Amputees are able to feel warmth and cold, pressure and pain, in the lost limb. One man described the delight of being able to feel the warmth of his wife's hand after more than a decade.

• • •

Your entire skeleton is replaced every seven years.

• • •

It requires the use of 72 muscles to speak a single word.

• • •

There are no muscles in your fingers. All movement is powered by muscles in your arms, attached to the tendons in your fingers.

• • •

Your toenails contain trace amounts of gold. No one knows why.

• • •

The ethmoid bone between your eyes contains trace amounts of magnetite, also known as lodestone, which some think helps you navigate. People with an innate sense of direction can point north, even if blindfolded and disoriented. The magnetite in their sinuses may give them this ability.

Similar deposits of magnetite have been found in the heads of dolphins, tuna, salmon, pigeons, and honeybees, all of which navigate, some over vast distances.

• • •

The temperature of your hands and feet can be 40 degrees below normal without causing lasting harm.

• • •

Your fingers and toes get all wrinkly in the bathtub because your skin absorbs water like a sponge. There are no fat-secreting glands in the hands and feet, so they tend to absorb water, swell, and wrinkle.

OUR PERSONAL ZOOS

Healthy clean skin has about 5 million microbes to the square inch (2.5 cm × 2.5 cm). Spit contains between 10 million and a billion bacteria to the mouthful. Every time you defecate, you lose 100,000 million microbes, but they are quickly replaced.

• • •

A tiny creature less than one-fourth the size of the period at the end of this sentence lives out its entire life cycle on your face. Large populations of follicle mites eat, mate, lay eggs, and die within a small patch of skin. Their favorite home is your eyebrows, and no amount of scrubbing or shaving will remove them.

• • •

Every day, every one of us sheds millions and millions of skin cells, which become dust in a never-ending cascade. By the time you reach age 70, you will have shed 40 pounds of dead skin. This dust is eaten by harmless dust mites that consume the flaked-off pieces of us like so many tiny vacuum cleaners. Dust mites live literally everywhere people do, and we sleep peacefully with them every night. The only conflict arises when some people develop an allergy to inhaling the mites.

• • •

Several species of bacteria live around your eyes.

• • •

Your body can be compared to an aquarium: mostly water, about 10 gallons (38 litres) of it, with billions of bacteria and independent organisms living and breeding inside us.

• • •

The human body is host to a wide range of living organisms. Most are harmless, some are beneficial, and a very few (numerically speaking) are harmful. Those viruses that sicken or kill us can be seen as newcomers, not yet adapted to cohabitation, as it is bad news to kill your host. So where do the plagues come from? And how can they cover the earth so quickly? The Black Death of the 13th century, the Spanish Flu of the early 20th century, AIDS in the 1980s and 1990s—where did these viruses come from? The astronomers Fred Hoyle and Chandra Wickramasinghe believe that they come from outer space. Regular invasions of new viral infections, they believe, arrive in the dust of comets.

PEOPLE ARE STRANGER THAN YOU THINK

Every one of us started out as an egg the size of the period at the end of this sentence. An adult human has about 100 trillion cells. Every single cell contains all the information needed to make another you.

• • •

If you lose 80% of your liver, it will still function, and it will grow back within a few months.

• • •

Children under the age of ten have been known in rare cases to grow back thumbs and fingers.

• • •

The antiseptic conditions of present-day hospitals are less than 150 years old. Before that, many women died of ''childbed fever'' because doctors delivered their babies without washing their hands after performing autopsies or visiting another bedside.

A different approach was used by a Dr. Addinell Hewson in 1872. He treated 93 patients with gunshot wounds, burns, open sores, and new surgical scars, by packing the wounds with *dirt.* He claimed they all responded well. Hewson's results were dismissed at the time, but he may have been on to something. Helpful bacteria live in soil, a fact that was not rediscovered for more than 50 years.

• • •

A one-year-old girl in Chicago contracted sleeping sickness. For weeks she hovered between life and death; then she started to recover. She was partially paralyzed and her personality had changed. She was sullen and morose, having previously been playful and happy. She ripped up her toys, screamed, and had convulsions, ten to twenty a day. The doctors consulted and decided on a risky operation. Since it seemed one half of her brain was responsible, they removed the right half of the girl's brain on May 14, 1951. Within three weeks she showed great improvement. The remaining half of her brain had taken over all functions. Her convulsions ended and her sunny personality was restored.

• • •

A mathematics student at Sheffield University, England, had an IQ of 126, well above average, excellent grades, and appeared normal in every way. So it was a shock to his neurologist to find he had virtually no brain whatsoever. Technically he was hydrocephalic. His skull was filled with cerebrospinal fluid and just a tiny fraction of an inch of brain tissue. Most hydrocephalics are severely retarded and die within months of birth. The doctor, Professor John Lorber, has since identified several hundred other intelligent people with the same baffling condition.

• • •

In recent years there has been a lot of talk about left brain and right brain and the differences between them. The left brain is responsible for intellect, logic, language, and concrete thinking. The right brain controls intuition, emotions, and abstract thinking. But the differences go beyond that. The left brain recognizes familiar faces, remembers names, and recalls solutions that worked to solve problems. The right brain follows a storyline, understands a punchline, interprets tone of voice, makes metaphors, follows directions, and suggests creative solutions. You speak with your left brain but sing with your right.

• • •

The average person has near total recall of visual memories. Names, words, and numbers are harder to remember, no matter our age. This leads scientists to believe we have separate storage sites for visual memories and linguistic ones. Experiments show visual images are stored directly, while words have to be decoded, sorted, and recoded by the brain. That's why it's so hard to match the name to the face.

• • •

Alpha waves are recorded when you are in a state of relaxed awareness, awake but with your eyes closed. Beta waves are given off when you are fully alert, concentrating on a mental activity. The slow theta waves occur both in sleeping people who are dreaming and during creative thinking. Delta waves occur when you are deeply asleep or under anaesthetic.

• • •

Peter Fairley, investigator of premonitions, states that when people who score above chance in ESP are tested, more often than not they begin to feel they are good at it. Soon they start applying conscious thought to their decisions, which destroys the accuracy of the results. "Basically an alpha rhythm comes through only when the person being investigated is doing or thinking practically nothing. It disappears the moment they try to do something or make some mental effort. If there is such a thing as premonition, I reckon it's in some way connected with the alpha rhythm of the brain," Fairley states.

• • •

Everyone knows there are two kinds of tiredness—physical exhaustion and mental or emotional fatigue. Not surprisingly, there are two kinds of sleep needed to recover from them. REM (rapid eye movement) sleep is a deep, dream-filled sleep that produces special chemicals that repair damaged nerve cells in the brain, the kind that are damaged by stress or prolonged mental effort. So REM sleep is good for mental fatigue. SWS (slow wave sleep) restores the physical body by replacing the supplies of proteins and chemicals that the body uses up in activity. Everyone needs about the same amount of SWS sleep, about 5 to $5\frac{1}{2}$ hours, while some people require extra REM sleep to catch up.

• • •

The Greek philosopher Aristotle felt that the brain was not the site of intellectual activity. He thought it was an organ for cooling the blood.

• • •

The volume of blood that reaches the brain changes drastically when a person receives a telepathic message. This interesting discovery was made by electrochemist Douglas Dean. In one case, a message was sent 1200 miles from New York, producing a change in the blood volume of the receiver in Florida.

• • •

Conventional theory holds that memories are stored as electrical impulses in the brain, but scientists have been unable to locate memory storage areas. Instead, memories are retained even if large parts of the brain are damaged, suggesting that memories are somehow retained throughout the brain. British biochemist Rupert Sheldrake suggests the brain is a device for tuning in memories through "morphic resonance." Science has not come up with a way of measuring this, but it may be a solution to paranormal phenomena. If we can tune in to our own memories, why not someone else's (telepathy) or their futures (clairvoyance)? Perhaps Carl Jung was right about a collective unconscious, a pool of wisdom and knowledge that all humans can tap into.

• • •

By age 60, your brain contains at least 4 times the information it did at age 21. But IQ tests do not reflect this, as the accumulated wisdom helps you make judgments based on experience, something standardized tests do not measure. Your vocabulary triples between age 25 and 45. But your short-term memory diminishes after age 30.

• • •

Introverts lose their memory faster than extroverts.

• • •

Humans are the only animals that weep. There is a difference in the chemistry of "reflex" tears (like from cutting onions) and emotional tears. Emotional tears have more protein-based hormones, including prolactin, and natural painkillers. Having a good cry really does make you feel better.

• • •

Liars have forced smiles. A forced smile is more noticeable on the left side of the face in right-handed people and vice-versa. Liars touch their faces a lot.

• • •

Seeing another person yawn makes it likely you will yawn yourself. No one knows why. Thinking about, even reading about, yawning can set you off. Persons with mental disorders such as psychoses rarely yawn. Yawning is now thought of as a way of stretching the facial muscles and ridding the body of excess carbon dioxide.

• • •

Schizophrenics have a certain chemical in their sweat that other people can smell. They can also smell hostility in other people.

• • •

Some patients who have seizures in their temporal lobes report smelling peculiar odors, hearing bizarre sounds, feeling mystical sensations, and seeing visions.

HUMAN STORIES

A house painter fell off a roof and was in a coma for two weeks. All the lines in his hands vanished. As he recovered, the lines on his hands gradually reappeared.

•   •   •

When Alice Little was in her twenties, she was dying of tuberculosis. She had always had a very short life line on her hands. One of her lungs was collapsed to prevent the disease from spreading to the other lung, but it spread anyway. The doctors told her there was nothing more they could do; but then a new drug, streptomycin, was put on the market, and she was among the first to try it. When she awoke after taking the first dose she looked at her hands; the rest of her life line had appeared overnight. My mother, Alice Little, lived another 35 years.

•   •   •

When the writer Anthony Burgess was 39, his doctors found a brain tumor and gave him a year to live. He made a vow to write

10 novels in that last year so his widow could live on the royalties. At the end of the year he had completed 5½ novels and the brain tumor had completely disappeared. He lived to age 76 and wrote about 50 novels and at least 15 nonfiction works. He was so prolific even his publisher was unsure of the exact number of his books at the time of his death.

• • •

The actor Dana Andrews was born in Dont, Mississippi, in 1909, to a Baptist minister with a large family. He went to work for an oil company. He had a secure job at the height of the Depression, in 1931, but he quit. Andrews spent all the money he had on a black alpaca trench coat, a white silk scarf, and a homburg hat, reasoning that in order to be successful, one must look the part. He hitchhiked to Los Angeles and eventually got his break in the movie business. He made more than 70 movies, including the classic *Laura* and *The Best Years of Our Lives*.

• • •

The writer Mark Twain had a profound psychic experience as a young man. At the time he was an apprentice riverboat pilot and his handsome younger brother Henry was a clerk on the same vessel, the *Pennsylvania*. In 1858 they sailed down the Mississippi and Twain had a dream. He dreamed his brother was killed in an accident. Henry was laid out in a metal coffin on two chairs, with a bouquet of white flowers on his chest, a single red flower in the center of the bouquet. The dream was so vivid Twain awoke in a panic, and was mentally preparing himself to tell their mother when he realized it was a dream. He confided in his sister and tried to talk to Henry about what to do if there was an accident.

In New Orleans, Twain was transferred to another riverboat

for the return trip. The *Pennsylvania*'s boilers exploded below Memphis. Henry was not killed outright, but he was badly scalded and Mark Twain was at his bedside when he died. He went to the hall where several victims of the accident were laid out, all but one in plain pine boxes. The ladies of the town had taken pity on Henry because of his youth and beauty and had purchased a metal coffin for him. Exactly like in the dream, it was resting on two chairs. The only missing element was the flowers. As Twain sat grieving, an elderly woman came in carrying a bouquet of white flowers with a single red rose and laid it on the dead man's chest.

• • •

Edgar Allan Poe wrote in 1837 a horrific tale of a disaster at sea called *The Narrative of Arthur Gordon Pym*. In the story, four sailors are shipwrecked and are adrift in a small lifeboat. They run out of food, and starving, draw straws to see who will be killed and eaten by the others. The cabin boy, Richard Parker, loses and is stabbed to death and cannibalized.

A shipwreck more than forty years later set four sailors adrift in an open boat. Starving, they did draw straws and they killed and ate one of their company. The unlucky sailor was named Richard Parker and he was the cabin boy. The three surviving sailors stood trial for Parker's murder in 1884. The macabre coincidence (or psychic precognition?) was reported to the *London Sunday Times* by a Nigel Parker, whose great-grandfather's cousin had been eaten.

• • •

A Russian named Bernard Kajinsky was jolted awake in 1919 by the sound of a spoon hitting glass. The next morning Kajinsky learned his best friend had died in the night of typhus. At the moment of his death, his friend's mother was about to give him a dose of medicine, but instead had dropped the spoon into the glass, producing a distinctive ringing sound.

• • •

Betty Fox was the wife of an impoverished blacksmith in Shropshire, England, in 1892. One morning she told her family that she'd had a strange dream. She watched some men in odd uniforms bury something furtively by the side of the road. They looked about nervously but did not see her. She described the men as like ancient warriors in battle gear: bronze helmets, knee-length skirts, sandals, and carrying thick round metal shields. The next night Fox had a similar dream and recognized the road.

Betty Fox's family laughed at her. She had the dream again, and this time she decided to act on it. She brought a spade and walked along the road until she recognized landmarks. Following her instincts, she dug under a large bush. Within a few minutes she unearthed some ancient gold coins. Fox kept digging and uncovered an earthenware pot filled with gold and silver coins. She brought the treasure to her family, but they feared it would be seized by the Crown. They sold one coin to a local collector named Oatley. He recognized it as being Roman in origin, and after learning its origins, assured the Foxes the treasure was theirs to sell. They sold it to a professional archeologist for a small fortune. Betty Fox then took the archeologist to the place, and this led to the rediscovery of the ancient Roman town of Uriconium, lost for more than 1500 years.

• • •

One of the stories of disappearances that regularly turns up in schoolchildren's history books is the story of the Lost Colony of

Virginia. The tiny colony of 120 hardy souls was established in 1587 on an island off Virginia, and the first Christian child in America, Virginia Dare, was born there. The colony soon ran into trouble, however, and relief from England was delayed 3 years by a war with Spain. When relief ships finally arrived, they found no one there. The only clue to their whereabouts was the single word "CROATOAN," carved on a post.

The Croatoans were a friendly Indian tribe, also known as the Hatteras Indians. The most credible theory yet advanced to the fate of the Roanoke Islanders is that they sought refuge from hostile tribes and hunger among their friends the Croatoans and eventually intermarried. The Hatteras Indians told historian John Lawson in 1709 that some of their ancestors were white people.

More than a century after the Lost Colony disappeared, trappers entered a wild area in Robinson, North Carolina, and found to their amazement a large group of Indians with white skin and blue or grey eyes, who spoke English. The family names of these people were the same as many of the colonists, and it was said "...they use phrases of speech that have scarcely been heard since the days of Shakespeare."

• • •

Another story concerns an English surveying party exploring what is now Missouri, just after the American Revolution. The party visited the camp of Mandan Indians. When the officer in charge spoke to his orderly in Welsh, all present were astonished when a Mandan responded in Welsh too. They compared notes and discovered about half the Mandan language was identical with Welsh. In addition, many of the natives were fair-skinned and had blue or grey eyes.

A Prince Madoc of Wales sailed west in 1170 and was never heard from again. According to one theory, he may have sailed into the Gulf of Mexico, up the Mississippi, and become assimilated into the Mandan tribe. The true story will probably never be known as the Mandans were wiped out by diseases brought by the Europeans and none remain.

• • •

Byron Somes was a newspaperman for the *Boston Globe* in August 1883, and he was a heavy drinker. He passed out at his desk and had a terrible nightmare. He witnessed a volcano exploding, rivers of lava, tidal waves, and the deaths of thousands of people. He awoke in a cold sweat and wrote down some of what he'd seen in the dream. He staggered home and didn't show up for work for days. His editor found the notes on his desk, marked "Important."

Thousands of miles away, Krakatoa erupted in the largest explosion in modern history. It was heard in Japan and Australia. A 50-foot (15-metre) tidal wave killed those spared by the explosion, the fiery lava, and the poisonous gases released by the volcano. Communications were primitive in those days and what there was in Java and Sumatra was wiped out. The editor at the *Globe* decided Somes's notes were about Krakatoa, so he ran a detailed story based on them, which other newspapers in turn picked up.

When Somes was located, his editor demanded more information. He admitted it was all a dream. They were debating whether or not to publish a public apology when more information arrived. Byron Somes's dream was completely accurate. One detail that hadn't been published was that he heard the word "Pralape" over and over. Years later he came across the word in some Dutch historical society papers. It was the ancient native name for Krakatoa.

• • •

The nonfiction author Charles Berlitz was stationed in Panama in 1943. His mother became ill and was hospitalized in New York City. Berlitz wanted badly to visit her but could not get leave. He fell asleep one afternoon and dreamed he went to the hospital. Berlitz entered, signed his name at the register, got on the elevator, pushed the button for his mother's floor, then awoke. It was 1:15 P.M., Panama time.

A few days later, Berlitz got a letter from his mother. She said a nurse had told her that her son had arrived for a visit, but he never got to her room. The nurse and the receptionist had seen him get on the elevator, but no one saw him get off. The register showed his signature, and the time, 12:15 P.M., New York time.

• • •

A Spanish soldier reported for duty to the palace in Manila, the Philippines, on October 25, 1593. The next thing he knew, he appeared in the main plaza of Mexico City, 9000 miles (14,400 km) away. His odd uniform quickly drew a crowd, and he was thrown in jail. The baffled soldier could offer no explanation. All he knew was that the governor of Manila had been assassinated the night before, and he had been ordered to the palace. Confirmation came by ship months later and the unfortunate man was shipped back to the Philippines.

• • •

A Portuguese soldier was in the colony of Goa, India, in 1655. The man was transported by an unknown agency back to Portugal, and he could offer no explanation for his arrival. The

Inquisition charged him with witchcraft, as it was well known that only witches could fly. He was burned at the stake.

• • •

When John Snell of Poole, England, was 25, he consulted an Indian palm reader. The Indian told him he would die on his 45th birthday. For 20 years Snell put the warning in the back of his mind. He became a truck driver and a hard drinker. After his 44th birthday, though, it began to bother him. He quit drinking and when his birthday rolled around, he refused to leave the house. The local newspaper reported the death of John Snell of Poole on his 45th birthday. But it was a *different* John Snell, a neighbor, who had died, not the one whose palm was read all those years before.

• • •

In 1957, a doctor made a house call on the Oakins family in London. He noticed an old man sitting motionless in a corner. "Who's that?" the doctor asked. "Oh, that's just old Uncle Toby," was the answer. "He wound down like a clock one day and hasn't moved since." The doctor examined the unfortunate Uncle Toby, who had been left in that corner, like a houseplant, for seven years. He was cold to the touch, barely breathing, and had a faint pulse. Once removed to a hospital, his malfunctioning thyroid was treated, and Uncle Toby returned to the land of the living. He remembered nothing of the years he had lost and thought he had been ill a day or two. Ironically, he died just six weeks later, the victim of a malignant cancer that had been reawakened as well.

• • •

A Cajun named Shep joined a fishing trip off Hawaii. He fell down a hatchway and was badly injured. Paralyzed and in severe pain, Shep thought of a close friend, a woman named Milly. The time of the accident was 9:12 P.M.

At the same time, Milly was visiting the wife of Shep's captain. The wife, a Samoan woman, suddenly felt a tremendous blow to the head and fell into a sort of trance. She came out of it saying that something terrible had happened on her husband's boat. Milly took note of the time: 9:14 P.M.

According to parapsychologist Lyall Watson, apparently the telepathic message from Shep to Milly had hit a sort of cultural "busy signal." The message was received instead by another woman who happened to be nearby, and whose Samoan culture may have made her more receptive.

• • •

Ambrose Brennan III, a pastor at Deliverance Temple Church in Shippensburg, Pennsylvania, had just sat down to dinner at 9:30 P.M., when a feeling told him to go back to his church. When he arrived, he saw a young girl rush from the church and head toward the train tracks. Recognizing her as a parishoner he had counseled for depression, he chased after her. Pastor Brennan was just in time to tackle her and save her from being hit by a train.

• • •

Mrs. Hazel Lambert was making a routine trip to the grocery store in Pennsbury Heights, Pennsylvania, in December 1958. She felt an overwhelming compulsion to speed down a street she had never taken before. Mrs. Lambert was barely in time to see a child's red mittens gripping the ice of the canal. Without hesitation, she drove off the road and onto the ice. The car started to sink and Mrs. Lambert honked and yelled for help. Two men arrived in time to rescue both the lady and the

2-year-old girl, who would almost certainly have drowned if not for the woman's strange compulsion.

•　•　•

Judge Edmonds of the New York Supreme Court and his daughter Laura were having guests for tea. Laura spoke only English and a smattering of schoolgirl French. Among the guests was a Greek gentleman, Mr. Evangedides, who had never before been in their house. As soon as she laid eyes on him, Laura went up to him and spoke earnestly to him in Greek. He turned pale and burst into tears. He explained that she had told him his son was dead and that he knew it was true as she spoke in the voice of a friend who was dead. He left. Laura remembered nothing of the incident.

Her message was confirmed in a phone call from Evangedides the next day.

•　•　•

One day in 1955, a little girl named Joicey Hurth of Cedarburg, Wisconsin, came home from a birthday party. Her mother told her that her father and brother had left without her to go to the movies a block and a half away, and the girl dashed down the street to join them. Mrs. Hurth was washing dishes a few minutes later when she felt a powerful apprehension that her daughter had been in an accident. Without another thought she picked up the phone and called the theater. "My little girl was on her way there," she said, "she has had an accident. Is she badly hurt?" The employee was amazed and said, "It just happened! How did you know?" Joicey Hurth had indeed run into the path of a car. She was bruised and shaken but not badly hurt. Immediately after being struck, Joicey had cried out in her mind, "Mama, Mama, Mama!"

Apparently her mother "heard" her.

• • •

Fred Trusty of Painesville, Ohio, was building steps into a hill in his backyard when a "strange feeling" made him look at a nearby pond. He saw a ripple in the water and did a double take. This time he saw a little boy's cap floating in the water. Trusty dashed to the pond in time to save his own 2-year-old son.

• • •

Doctor Edward Gibson Moon was making daily visits to his patient, Lord Edward Carson, on the Isle of Thanet in the early 1930s. The patient's mansion was screened from the road by a tall hedge; the house was connected to the road with a semicircular driveway.

Dr. Moon, who considered himself a rational man of science, had an odd experience while paused in thought on the front steps one morning. He glanced up toward the hedge and was startled to see the hedge had completely vanished. He looked about in confusion but could not see a single familiar landmark. Instead of a paved road, a muddy track stretched through empty fields. Odder still, a strangely dressed man approached. He was carrying a flintlock rifle, and wearing breeches, riding boots, a caped overcoat, and a top hat with a narrow crown. The stranger stopped and the two men stared at each other. Then Dr. Moon turned around to see if the house was still there. It was. When he looked back, the hedge and the paved road had reappeared and the man from the 18th century had vanished.

• • •

In 1957, two Englishwomen were vacationing near Dieppe, on the coast of France. Their sleep was shattered one night by the unmistakable sounds of a raging battle. They heard artillery, explosions, bombers droning overhead, and the cries and screams of wounded and dying men. The gunfire began just before 4 A.M. and stopped abruptly at 4:50 A.M. At first light, the two ladies tried to find out what was going on. To their astonishment, there had been no battle and no one else had heard a thing.

On August 19, 1942, the Allies had landed in a bloody practice invasion at Dieppe. The shelling had started at 3:47 A.M. and stopped abruptly at 4:50 A.M. The two Englishwomen heard the entire invasion, fifteen years later.

• • •

A physician named Edward E. Rowell Jr. disappeared from his home in Stamford, Connecticut, on May 25, 1915. Dr. Rowell was a victim of amnesia; he regained his memory six weeks later, as he looked down at his bleeding, blistered hands. He was working as a ditchdigger in a gravel pit in Indiana, with no idea how he'd gotten there.

• • •

A British soldier named C. H. Peachey was wounded in the head in World War I. After an operation, he could remember nothing. He wandered the United States from one mental hospital to another. After 10 years, he was operated on again and awoke with his memory restored. He returned to England, but found his wife had remarried and his children had been adopted. But his deaf-mute brother was so startled to see Peachey alive that his powers of speech and hearing were miraculously restored.

• • •

Captain de Montalt was in a dugout with a dozen other officers on New Year's Eve 1916–1917, when they heard the whine of a shell directly overhead. He just had time to thrust one arm in a sleeve of a coat when the shell exploded. He awoke in a hospital with no memory of who he was. Doctors could only tell him that papers in the coat identified him as a Canadian named de Montalt. The captain married and lived happily for a while in England, until one night in a London restaurant he heard Swedish being spoken and he realized he could understand every word.

It took some research, but de Montalt tracked down an army publication listing all the Swedish officers of World War I. He was drawn to the name Gustaf Duner; so he wrote to the address listed and found his long-lost mother and brother. He was Gustaf Duner, thought dead 7 years, and the coat belonged to de Montalt, who had been killed in the explosion.

• • •

In February 1940, Warren Felty was driving home to Middletown, Pennsylvania. He saw the car ahead of him skid and go off the road into a snowbank near Camp Hill. Felty found the driver had been thrown through the windshield, so he drove him to Harrisburg Hospital. The injured man's name was William Miller, and they became acquainted after he recovered.

In an odd coincidence, both men joined the Army Air Force, and both became B-17 pilots. Unbeknownst to both, they were both shot down and taken prisoner in Germany in 1944. Along with 4000 other POWs, they were herded ahead of the advancing Russian Army in the bitter winter of 1944. Many froze to death on the forced march. Warren Felty saw a man in a snowbank and kicked him to keep him moving. He said later, "There he was, Bill Miller. Unbelievable." Once again, Felty pulled him from a snowbank and saved his life. Both survived the war and in 1986 they celebrated their fortunate friendship.

THE SENSES

Humans can hear between 16 and 40,000 cycles per second. If we could hear at lower frequencies than that, we could pick up the sound of our own muscles working.

• • •

Loud noise makes the pupils dilate. Surgeons and watchmakers and others who do delicate work have found that a noisy environment will make their eyes go out of focus.

• • •

High-frequency sounds make the skin more sensitive.

• • •

Women have better hearing than men, especially in the high pitch ranges. A sound above 85 decibels sounds *twice* as loud to a woman as to a man. Women listen better and remember what they hear better.

• • •

Loss of hearing is *not* a natural part of growing old. People who live in quiet environments, like the Bushmen of the Kalahari, have excellent hearing in old age. Bushmen can hear airplanes 70 miles (112 km) away. A Stone Age people of the Sudan called the Mabaan were discovered in 1956. They traditionally spoke in whispers, never shouted, did not use drums or guns, and their hearing was spectacular. It was better at all ages than any other human hearing ever examined.

Exposure to noise is what causes us to go deaf. Loud noise flattens the delicate hairs in the inner ear, and eventually they will not stand up again.

• • •

Of the five senses, smell is the first to diminish with age.

• • •

Most people, if asked, will deny the ability, but if they try, they can distinguish whether a piece of clothing was worn by a man or a woman simply by the way it smells.

• • •

Mothers of schoolchildren can find their child's T-shirt by its smell. Fathers do not have this ability.

• • •

Some scientists speculate that women have better smell and taste reception than men because it is a survival skill. If they could detect whether a potential food source was spoiled or poisonous, their senses could save lives.

• • •

The sense of taste cannot operate unless saliva is mixed with the food. If you place salt or sugar on a dry tongue you cannot taste it.

• • •

Recent evidence shows that saliva has pain-killing and infection-fighting properties; so the urge to suck a wound is beneficial after all.

• • •

By age ten, the tens of thousands of taste buds that originally covered your throat and the roof of your mouth cease functioning, although the taste buds on the surface of the tongue remain functional.

• • •

The scent left by a barefoot human is actually strong enough for another human to follow the trail.

• • •

Body odor in Asian people is much less strong than in whites and blacks, because they have fewer sweat glands and are less hairy. An offensive body odor in Japanese men was once grounds for disqualification for military service, since it was so unusual.

• • •

Albinos have a poor sense of smell. Dark-skinned individuals have keener noses.

• • •

Helen Keller claimed she could distinguish her visitor's occupations by the scents that clung to them. "When a person passes quickly from one place to another, I get a scent impression of where he has been—the kitchen, the garden, or the sickroom,'' Keller said. She called the sense of smell the "fallen angel of the senses'' because it is ignored and taken for granted.

• • •

Women who were given musk to smell in an international flavors and fragrances experiment ovulated more frequently and conceived with greater ease.

• • •

Collection rates increased 14 percent in England after bill collectors scented their bills with a sex attractant.

• • •

Dr. Gary Schwartz of Yale University found the odor of spiced apples produced a pleasant relaxation response in stressed individuals, lowering their blood pressure considerably.

• • •

Real estate agents have found that sprinkling cinnamon in a pan and heating it in the oven will help sell a home.

• • •

Aromatherapy is gaining new believers after many years of neglect in Western culture. The Greeks, the pharaohs of Egypt, and the Chinese all used the distilled essence of flowers, herbs, and other plants for their beneficial qualities. Even the Three Wise Men, according to the interpretations of aromatherapists, brought gifts of therapeutic qualities to the baby Jesus. The smell of frankincense brings feelings of faith, inspiration, inner strength, and a deeper connection with the spiritual; myrrh evokes feelings of confidence and stability and is useful for meditation. The third gift, gold, has no known aromatherapy benefits.

• • •

Tangerine is said to be a cheering scent. Marjoram, chamomile, jasmine, and vanilla soothe tension. Cinnamon, nutmeg, and peppermint relieve feelings of dizziness. Lemon, rosemary, and wintergreen help with headaches. Depression is eased by Borneo camphor, lavender, or verbena.

• • •

Japanese office workers get a jolt of lemon in their air conditioning units in the morning to wake them up. Lunchtime brings essence of rose to soothe and relieve anxiety, and in late afternoon, they are exposed to tea tree oil to perk things up again.

• • •

Some hotels in the Marriott chain in the United States are experimenting with aromatherapy to soothe their guests. The Sloan Kettering Cancer Center in New York scents the air in the rooms of magnetic resonance imaging machines with vanilla to relieve the stress of patients.

• • •

The threatening quality of a direct stare is well known. Some years ago, a department store owner installed a frieze of staring eyes to warn off shoplifters. It worked surprisingly well, and sales were not diminished.

• • •

When we look at an object, say, a yellow curtain, we see it as yellow. But in truth it is every color *but* yellow. Yellow is the color that was not absorbed and is reflected to our eyes.

• • •

The Jalé tribesmen of New Guinea are surrounded all their lives by every shade of green. There is no word for "green" in their language. They only need to distinguish shades by saying "light" or "dark."

• • •

Women see more shades of red than men do. They see better in the dark and have wider peripheral vision.

• • •

Color sensitivity diminishes with age. Blues look darker and yellows appear less bright but greens and oranges are less affected by the thickening of the eye lens. Aging painters choose less blue and violet, as they can no longer distinguish the differences.

• • •

The neurologist Oliver Sacks described an artist whose world was shattered after a car accident. The artist lost all perception of color. His entire world was reduced to black, white, and shades of grey. Sex was abhorrent, as skin color became "rat color." Food was disgusting-looking and gradually he turned to black and white foods like black olives and white rice, black coffee and yogurt, as they looked the most normal. His own dog looked so strange he considered buying a Dalmatian. His wife had to help him dress, which he found humiliating. Gradually he came to grips with his fate, as there was no treatment, and began painting the world as only he could see it.

• • •

Some blind people can see but do not know it. "Blindsight" is present in people whose blindness is caused by brain damage, rather than damage to the eyes themselves. Anthony Marcel researched patients with blindsight at Cambridge University. He put objects before them, then persuaded them to reach for the objects. The people said they could not see anything, yet they grasped the objects with a sureness that astonished everyone.

• • •

People blind since birth dream not in visual images but of sounds and textures. They may reach out to touch dream objects in their sleep.

• • •

Homer, the poet of the *Iliad* and the *Odyssey,* is said to have been blind. In 1955, a German researcher named von Schumann analyzed the dreams described in the epics and found they were almost all in imagery of sound and touch—exactly what a blind person would describe.

• • •

Canadian nurses have revived an ancient healing practice of laying on of hands. Over the last 15 years, over 5000 nurses have been trained in touch therapy, based on a theory that everyone has an energy field that can be felt and is symmetrical in healthy people. The nurse feels for blockages, or areas of heat and cold, in sick people. A program of gentle massage and physical therapy will restore the body's energy field. It is not a cure, but touch therapy eases pain, reduces stress, induces relaxation, and speeds healing.

• • •

Petting a dog or watching a fish tank is good for your health.

• • •

Synesthesia is a rare condition in which the senses are somehow combined. Synesthetes see words, taste colors and shapes, and feel flavors. Tastes, in one case, were felt in the synesthete's hand as round blobs, pointy objects, or tendrils. Sometimes a single event can start all the senses jangling. A bell ringing made one synesthete see a small round object roll across the floor; she felt a rough rope on her fingers; and she tasted salt water. It is not completely understood how this happens. People are born with the condition and it lasts all their lives. It may run in families.

One woman described why she liked her husband's laugh, because it was "a wonderful golden brown, with a flavor of crisp buttery toast." A man described the taste of mint as feeling like smooth cool glass columns.

A woman in Oklahoma saw the purring of a kitten as a long chain in the air. A telephone ringing looked like diamond-shaped blocks.

Several synesthetes of a particular physician reported seeing things when they heard certain sounds. A radiator clanking, the whoosh of an electric furnace, or the barking of a dog produced flashes of light, blobs, pulsing flowers, flames, or a jumble of images like a kaleidoscope.

S. V. Shereshevski was a professional memory expert. His secret was that he had synesthesia, and he experienced words with all his senses. Every word had a shape, color, texture, sound, taste, and even movement. So when a certain tone was played, he said it looked like pink fireworks, felt rough, and tasted like an oversalted pickle. With all these associations, remembering was easy.

YIN AND YANG

British psychologist Diane McGuinness found that women can see better in dim light and can tolerate bright light better than men. Men can read small print better.

• • •

At every age, women have better hearing than men. They also have more sensitive noses and taste buds.

• • •

Psychologist Gregory Nicosia found that male test subjects were more likely to show stress, break into a sweat, and beg to be let out when crowded together in a small room. Women showed no such anxiety.

• • •

The first telephone operators were all men. They soon proved to be too impatient and bad-tempered for the job, so they were quickly replaced by women.

• • •

Men have a greater range in IQ than women do. The stupidest men are stupider than the stupidest women, and the smartest men are smarter than the smartest women.

• • •

Men change their minds two to three times more often than women do, according to studies at Northwestern University. Women will take longer to reach a decision, but once made, are more likely to stick to it.

• • •

Women navigate by landmarks and visual memories. Men navigate by direction (north/south) and distance, and tend to be better at reading maps.

• • •

Girls and women of all different ages and cultures are better at interpreting body language, facial expressions, and tone of voice. When shown videotapes of garbled conversations, women could still figure out the emotional content of the conversation.

• • •

More women than men can sing in tune.

• • •

Females have better fine motor movement, which gives them greater dexterity and better handwriting. Estrogen helps this ability, and around ovulation, manual dexterity gets better.

• • •

Men have less stamina. They have shorter life spans and are more susceptible to major diseases. Men's muscles are bigger and stronger, but they work less efficiently than women's muscles. Men may be at a disadvantage in some contests of endurance.

• • •

Women have a lower center of gravity than men because of their wider hips and narrower shoulders. They have better balance, flexibility, stability, and grace.

• • •

Women can feel pain more acutely, but, oddly, they are better at enduring it.

• • •

Since the X chromosome carries many of the genes that control immunity, women have twice the immunity men do, because they have two X chromosomes. Sex-linked conditions like hemophilia and color blindness are not expressed because of the other X chromosome in women.

• • •

During the London blitz, 70 percent more men than women needed psychological help to cope with the terror and stress. In concentration camps in both world wars, men were much more likely to break down emotionally, at a rate of 70 to 1. Women may shriek at spiders, as they are culturally expected to do so. But in truly harrowing situations, women cope better than men.

• • •

A study of schoolchildren at the University of South Florida revealed boys are four times more likely than girls to have their attention wander from their work, to stop work to play, or to just sit and watch other kids.

• • •

In a recent poll, 74 percent of U.S. residents believe the United States would be better off if women held half the positions in power.

. . .

Only 20 percent of U.S. residents believe that men are better leaders than women.

. . .

Men are twice as likely as women to steal on the job; five times more likely to steal from their clients or customers; and ten times more likely to steal from their coworkers.

. . .

If chosen for logical reasons, women should have been the first astronauts. Women are smaller, lighter, use less oxygen and resources, and bear up better under stress. The eyes of women are better at picking out detail, like stars in the blackness of space. Women are in general healthier than men are, all of which makes them excellent candidates for space flight. But it took 22 years of U.S. space exploration before the first woman astronaut, Sally Ride, went into space.

. . .

Researchers at the University of Pennsylvania have concluded that the brains of men and women are not identical. The region that controls emotional responses is more active in women and the part that controls an action-oriented response is more developed in men. Men do better on tests in which they are asked to visualize what an object looks like if it is rotated. Women do better on tests of mental dexterity, such as sorting objects according to a principle they have to guess. Language is concentrated in the left hemisphere in men, but it is shared equally on both sides of the brain in women.

• • •

One of the more intriguing differences between men and women involves how they react to being in love. Women report feeling more euphoric, high, and carefree than men do. When a relationship goes sour, men take it harder than women do; they get more depressed, lonely, and have more difficulty remaining friends with a former lover. They are more likely to hide their feelings instead of talking or crying them out. More women end relationships than men do.

SEX

The Puritans in New England outlawed sex on Sundays. Taking this law to an illogical extreme, they punished parents whose children happened to be born on a Sunday, as it was thought they must have been conceived on one. Transgressors were heavily fined.

• • •

Until the law was mercifully repealed in 1987, an unmarried couple living together in Massachusetts could be taken to a public gallows and flogged 39 times each with nooses draped over their necks. The 1784 law was only repealed after the town of Sharon threatened to carry it out on two of its city employees.

• • •

The word "Victorian" is synonymous with sexual repression. "Victorian" medicine reached an extreme in the U.S. between 1870 and 1910. Doctors removed healthy, normal ovaries from thousands of women in order to "cure" them of everything from hysteria and irritability to insanity. The surgeon Dr. Robert

Battey reported his patients were "tractable, orderly, industrious, and cleanly" after their ovaries were removed. He and his followers passed around ovaries at medical society meetings.

• • •

Sylvester Graham was a self-styled doctor in the early 19th century. He felt that sex was bad for the health and promoted a diet to lower the sex drive. Graham crackers, which still bear his name, were part of the diet, though the recipe has been changed over the years. Graham inspired John Harvey Kellogg, who made breakfast cereal that supposedly curbed the desire to masturbate. He and his brother started the Kellogg cereal empire in 1906.

• • •

The Mormon practice of polygamy, allowing a man to have more than one wife, began when founder Joseph Smith had a "revelation from God" that virgins could not enter heaven. It is said that Smith's wife took a dim view of the revelation.

• • •

A Boston ship captain returned home after a 3-year voyage in the 1780s. He kissed his wife in public. He was made to sit in the stocks for two hours as punishment for "lewd and unseemly behavior."

• • •

Prostitutes in Venice during the 15th century were required by law to appear on their balconies topless. The law was designed to prevent confusion in the minds of the men of the city.

• • •

North Carolina state representative Henry Aldridge argued on the floor of the General Assembly in 1995 that women don't get pregnant when raped because "the juices don't flow" during a rape. He was trying to defeat state funding of abortions for poor women and rape victims when he made the preposterous claim.

• • •

State senators in Montana passed a bill in April 1995 that would require all homosexuals to register with the police, be photographed and fingerprinted, and have their names published. They reversed their position a day later after a storm of protests.

• • •

One in five U.S. residents has homosexual fantasies.

• • •

In a recent poll of 2,000 people taken in *Worth* magazine, 40 percent of U.S. residents spend more time thinking about money than they do about sex. Only 13 percent think about sex more.

• • •

The zoologist Desmond Morris calls human beings "the sexiest primates." He does so for the following reasons: human females can have sex year-round, not just when they are in heat; ovulation is concealed, so three-quarters of sexual activity has nothing to do with procreation; females have sex even when pregnant, unlike the other primates; and human females are the only primates to have intense orgasms. Humans have sex longer, more intensely, and more often than any ape or monkey.

• • •

Women have longer orgasms than men do, at times up to a full minute long.

• • •

Some women, about 10 percent, can ejaculate when they have an orgasm. The fluid produced is similar to semen from a man who has had a vasectomy.

• • •

It is possible for a man to ejaculate without an erection.

• • •

According to the *Journal of Applied Psychology,* cold showers increase sexual arousal.

• • •

A German scientist, Niels Birbaumer, studied the brain waves of a variety of people. He found those who were passionately in love had brain wave patterns similar to people with low IQ scores, even though the people in love were above average in intelligence. In other words, love makes you stupid.

• • •

Kissing is good for you. During a kiss, sebum is exchanged, which is secreted by the skin to keep it supple. Passionate kisses increase the amount of sebum released. The glands that make it are concentrated in the face, lips, and neck. The skin takes on a rosy glow from blood flow. Kissing acts as an antidepressant, boosts your immune system, and increases your metabolism to burn fat. And orgasms cure headaches.

• • •

The hormones that produce that dreamy euphoric feeling of being in love are produced in the pituitary gland. Sadly, patients who have had surgery on the pituitary or tumors in that small gland attached to the underside of the brain are unable to fall in love.

• • •

The male hormone testosterone is released into the blood when men think about sex, when they fight, exercise, win a competition, or watch violent TV programs. Some winning athletes have higher levels of testosterone than losing ones. Men in their sixties have blood levels of testosterone equivalent to 9-year-old boys, while the testosterone levels increase in women of age 60.

• • •

Prolonged darkness inhibits sexual activity, while sunlight invigorates it. The "third eye" or pineal gland deep in the brain responds to darkness by releasing melatonin, which dampens desire. Bright lights or time in the sun reverses this effect. The Inuit people of Labrador endure four months of total darkness and corresponding diminished sexual activity. In the summer, these Arctic people have four months of constant sunlight—and nine months later, an annual baby boom.

• • •

The production of the male sex hormone peaks in fall and winter, not when "the juices flow" in the spring.

• • •

An Italian student has claimed to have invented a condom that plays music if it breaks during use. The young man, Lino Missio, incorporated a microchip that will play Beethoven if the condom ruptures. Missio says he is considering a verbal warning to be included in the recording.

• • •

One of the best known aphrodisiacs is "Spanish fly," a concoction of ground up European beetles. Its powers are still in dispute, and many say it is dangerous. One woman in Provence (France) claimed she fed Spanish fly to her husband, who responded by making love to her 87 times in two nights and then became ill. They had intercourse 3 more times *during the medical examination,* then gangrene attacked his penis and he died.

. . .

A bank in Rhode Island announced there was a shortage of pennies because people hoard them. Customers responded with 3.3 million coins. One man claimed he stashed a penny in a jar every time he made love to his wife. He brought in 43,000 pennies, saved over a 34-year period. That means he had sex 3.5 times a *day.*

. . .

Soccer games in Laos have an unusual halftime show. After the players leave, two performers come out at opposite ends of the field. One is wearing a giant erect penis made of straw that covers the head and shoulders. The other is wearing a straw vulva costume of equal gigantic proportions.

Both performers are blinded by their brightly painted costumes and are dependent on the shouts of the crowd to guide them toward each other. The crowd, with mounting excitement, yells out directions until penetration is achieved.

. . .

When the *Dolphin* dropped anchor in Tahiti in 1767, the sailors found the natives were friendly, *very* friendly. In fact, all a sailor needed to have a native girl have sex with him was to give her an iron nail. There was no metal on the islands, so nails were prized. The men pried so many nails out of the ship it was in serious danger of falling to pieces, so the captain cancelled all shore leave. The Tahitians later claimed they were led to believe white men had sex freely and openly with everyone they met.

. . .

Guy de Maupassant, the French writer, was a sexual freak of nature. He once had a bookkeeper accompany him to a brothel to verify that he had six girls in an hour. Late in life he told a journalist, "I am a little out of the common sexually, for I can make my instrument stand whenever I please." The interviewer expressed his doubts, so de Maupassant simply said, "Look at my trousers." He died at age 43 from syphilis.

• • •

In ancient Greece, a young girl was made fit for marriage by losing her virginity to a statue. Her hymen was ruptured by the stone penis of the god Priapus. Since her first lover was a god, it was thought, she was then ready to marry a man.

• • •

The inhabitants of the rundown section of Rome known as the Trastevere claim to have more than 2,000 vulgar words to describe the sex organs.

• • •

Venetian society sank to levels of depravity in the late 1700s. It was considered a disgrace for a married society woman not to have a lover. Nuns in low-cut gowns fought over who would be mistress to the representative from the Vatican. The Abbe of the monastery lost all his money gambling, so he bet his clothes and lost those too. He returned to the monastery naked.

• • •

A strange case of mass hysteria happened in Malaya in 1976. The male population became convinced their penises were shrinking, after a rumor spread that eating Thai oranges caused the condition. The Malayan men became obsessed with the size of their sex organs and could not concentrate on anything else.

DID YOU KNOW?

People who report having had an unhappy childhood usually become happy adults. Many successful adults had a terrible time as children.

• • •

One out of every 1,000 strangers you encounter at random will have killed someone.

• • •

A researcher at Lake Forest College, Illinois, found that people with brown or green eyes are more strongly stimulated by violence, profanity, and nudity than blue-eyed people.

• • •

Juries are made up of twelve people because originally they were made up of representatives of every astrological sign.

• • •

Emergency room personnel are significantly more likely to try to revive patients that arrive dead on arrival if the patient is good-looking.

• • •

Criminal behavior may be partially explained by chemical imbalances. These imbalances may show up as abnormal concentrations of trace metals in the hair. Violent criminals have much more calcium, magnesium, sodium, potassium, copper, zinc, iron, manganese, phosphorus, lead, and cadmium in their hair samples than nonviolent ones. Chemist William J. Walsh found that two patterns of behavior were associated with chemical imbalances—Type A, superficially law-abiding but vicious when provoked; and Type B, a chronically antisocial type with a lengthy criminal record.

• • •

Children who are sexually abused may have damage to their immune systems and brain development. In one study, the abused children had very high stress hormones, which killed brain cells in the areas of logic and language. They also had more of an antibody that weakens the immune system. Abuse victims had brain waves as different from normal as those of Alzheimer's patients and schizophrenics.

The damage can be offset by "learning new ways of positive behavior and gaining comfort" according to psychologist Karin Meiselman.

• • •

Bioclimatologist Manfred Curry was studying the effects of weather on people. He found that individuals fall into two groups, Group W and Group C. Group W people thrive in cool or cold weather and suffer in the heat. Group C people get peevish in cold weather and bloom in warm or hot weather. Group W people have round heads, large eyes, full cheeks that are often dimpled, smooth foreheads, and full lips. The corners of their mouths usually turn up.

Group C people have long, angular heads, smaller eyes, taut cheeks, furrowed foreheads, and thin lips. Their lips are often pressed together and they turn down at the corners.

Curry found that many people bear a combination of features, and their reactions to temperature are mixed. The more pronounced the traits are, however, the more likely it is that their mate will be the opposite.

• • •

When doctors went on strike for a month in Israel, the death rate dropped by one half.

• • •

Conventional medical wisdom has held for years that stress causes ulcers. A courageous Australian doctor named Barry Marshall challenged convention when he found most of his ulcer patients had a particular bacterium in their stomach linings. He treated them with antibiotics and they got better. To prove his point, Dr. Marshall drank a culture of the bacterium and gave himself an agonizing case of gastritis; then he cured himself with antibiotics.

• • •

Men who diet constantly had double the rate of heart disease of those who never dieted. They also were more likely to have hypertension and diabetes than the nondieters. The survey suggests that losing weight and then gaining it back, over and over, is more harmful than if you just accept yourself as you are.

• • •

Red-hot chile peppers show a lot of promise in lessening pain. When applied as an ointment containing capsaicin, the peppers stimulated the production of substance P, which tells the brain something painful is happening. But then substance P gets depleted, and fewer pain signals are sent to the brain.

• • •

Hair grows slowest at night. It speeds up in the morning, slows in afternoon, and grows faster again in the evening. Hair grows faster in summer than in winter. Hair on a man's head lives about three to five years; on a woman's, about seven years.

• • •

United States residents who did not graduate from high school are more likely to be smokers, to be overweight, and to live sedentary lives. As a group, better educated people live longer, regardless of race.

• • •

There are four basic parenting styles: authoritative, authoritarian, indulgent, and disengaged, according to psychology professor and author Laurence Steinberg and parent educator and author Nancy Samalin. The best parents are authoritative. They are warm and affectionate, set reasonable limits, and are responsive to the changing needs of growing children. The authoritative parents give their children many opportunities to make choices, so they learn from their mistakes. The child of these parents is confident, well-adjusted, a self-starter, and a creative problem-solver.

Authoritarian parents are stern and controlling, have many rules and punishments, and strive to have power over their children. The child of authoritarian parents is good at following orders and is eager to please, but may be moody, sulky, fearful, and susceptible to peer pressure.

Indulgent parents cannot bear to see their children unhappy. They are apt to give in easily, bargain, give the child too much freedom, or change the limits and rules frequently. The child of indulgent parents is unsettled, insecure, and may be self-centered, with little respect for authority. The relationships this child forms are superficial and short-lived.

Disengaged parents are cold and uninvolved. They are neglectful and let others make the decisions in their child's life. Children of disengaged parents have low self-esteem and feel that since their parents do not love them, they are unlovable. They may become rebellious and manipulative to get attention, may have trouble with the law, and may turn to alcohol and drugs.

ARTISTS AND THEIR ILK

Pablo Picasso was born dead. His midwife left him on a table. Picasso's uncle brought him to life with a lungful of cigar smoke.

• • •

Lord Byron, the poet, owed his existence to a curious set of circumstances. His mother, Miss Catherine Gordon of Gight, saw a play in Edinburgh called *Isabella, or the Fatal Marriage.* The young lady was overcome with emotion and cried out, "Oh my Biron! My Biron!" after a character in the play. A gentleman named John Byron heard of this, presented himself to her, and within a year they were married.

When Lord Byron was at Cambridge, there was a university rule against students keeping cats or dogs, so Byron kept a pet bear in his rooms.

• • •

The poet Alfred Tennyson went to Oxford to receive an honorary literary degree. He appeared dishevelled, with unruly hair to his shoulders and rumpled clothes. A voice from the gallery asked, "Did your mother call you early, dear?"

• • •

The lead singer in a production of *Lohengrin* was delayed in his entrance because the swans, which were to ferry him, were being pulled too quickly. Turning to a stage hand, he asked, "Can you tell me when the next swan leaves?"

• • •

Poet and artist William Blake and his wife liked to sit in their garden buck naked and recite poetry to each other, scandalizing the neighbors.

• • •

The novelist D. H. Lawrence liked to take off all his clothes and climb mulberry trees.

• • •

Robert Burton, author of *The Anatomy of Melancholy,* would relieve his own melancholia by going to a bridge at Oxford to listen to the bargemen swear at each other.

• • •

According to a recent study by Colin Martindale of the University of Maine, half of the 52 French and English poets he studied were psychotic and 15 percent were psychopaths. Percy Shelley, for instance, frequently had hallucinations of a man threatening him with a revolver.

• • •

People who suffer intense migraine headaches sometimes experience a phenomenon called "the aura" beforehand. Twenty minutes before the headache hits, the victim may see visions, flashing lights, intense colors, and apparitions. Lewis Carroll is said to have been inspired by the monsters he saw in the aura to create characters in *Alice in Wonderland.*

• • •

Ludwig van Beethoven poured ice water on his head when he was composing, to stimulate his brain.

• • •

Novelist Charles Dickens always aligned his bed to face north. He also faced north when he wrote.

• • •

The French writer Voltaire drank 50 cups of coffee a day.

• • •

The physicist Richard Feynman drove his wife crazy by playing bongo drums at night when he was working on a problem; finally, she divorced him.

• • •

French novelist Marcel Proust locked himself in a cork-lined room to minimize distractions.

• • •

The American writer Jack London (1876–1916) had an adventurous youth. In later years he took to his bed and did all his writing there.

• • •

British novelist and critic Aldous Huxley did not go blind, but his eyesight worsened in his later years. He learned Braille to compensate, and said one of the pleasures that came with the skill was to be able to read in bed with his arms under the covers and the light off.

• • •

Henry James' novel *The Ambassadors* was published in 1903 by Harper and Brothers. Neither the publisher nor the meticulous James nor the hundreds of people who presumably read the novel noticed for 47 years that Chapter 29 preceded Chapter 28. Henry James even came out with a revised edition in 1907, in which he moved commas around and changed a word here and there without noticing the glaring error.

At last a literary critic named Robert E. Young noticed in 1950 that characters acted in a peculiar fashion and displayed an amazing foreknowledge of events. He wrote a paper exposing the error. In 1955, Harper and Brothers came out with a "corrected" reprint, but mysteriously, Chapter 29 still came before Chapter 28. Finally a correct version was published, 39 years after the death of the author.

• • •

When Robert Graves finished his book *The White Goddess,* he sent it to an editor. The editor rejected it, then died of a heart attack within a month. A second editor also rejected the book and soon after hanged himself, wearing women's clothing. T. S. Eliot accepted the manuscript for publication and then won the Nobel Prize.

• • •

The lyricist of the song "Keep the Home Fires Burning," Lena Gilbert Ford, burned to death in her home.

•   •   •

The composer of "Home Sweet Home," John Howard Payne, spent most of his life on the road and died homeless in a foreign land.

•   •   •

W. C. Fields rose to prominence from a life of grinding poverty. Like many others, he retained a lifelong fear of losing all his money, so as he traveled from town to town, he would open bank accounts under ludicrous assumed names. He told one friend he had more than 700 bank accounts around the world, under names like Phineas T. Snodgrass. Naturally this created problems when it came time to settle Fields' estate. Many of these accounts may still remain open, waiting for rightful heirs to claim the money.

•   •   •

The largest and most perfect pearl was known as *La Peregrina* (the Wanderer). It was found in the 16th century by a slave and over the centuries was owned by Prince Philip of Spain, Mary Tudor of England, and the Bonapartes, among other notables. In January 1969 the actor Richard Burton bought the pearl for his wife, Elizabeth Taylor, at a cost of £15,400. Liz's dog found it on the shag carpet of their hotel suite in Las Vegas and chewed it up. La Peregrina is now worthless.

•   •   •

Soldiers of the conquistador Francisco Pizarro found raw emeralds in Peru the size of pigeon eggs. In the mistaken belief that real emeralds could not be broken, they smashed them with hammers and then discarded them.

•   •   •

The painter Marc Chagall made all his purchases by check. He discovered that his signature was so valuable that they were very rarely cashed, so he essentially got everything for free.

• • •

The famous Gilbert Stuart portrait of George Washington with the unfinished grey background was intentionally unfinished. Stuart kept it in his studio and copied it over and over to make more money. He left it unfinished so he could tell Martha Washington it wasn't done yet.

• • •

The artist Paul Cézanne taught his parrot to repeat the phrase "Cézanne is a great painter!" over and over.

• • •

Two artists lived in New Bedford, Massachusetts, and met occasionally on walks along the coast. One was a dabbler named Frederic Thompson, the other an acclaimed landscape painter named Robert Swain Gifford. In 1905, Thompson began feeling an overwhelming desire to paint landscapes in the style of his friend. He wandered into an art gallery and saw a sign promoting the display of the works of the *late* R. Swain Gifford. The shock of learning of the artist's death caused Thompson to black out into a fugue state, and he heard a voice say, "You see what I have done. Go on with the work." Thompson's personality changed and he seemed on the verge of mental collapse. He pulled himself together and started to work.

Thompson began a sketch of five isolated trees on a coast, then visited the artist's widow. His sketch exactly matched an unfinished painting Gifford had been working on when he died. Thompson's career spanned another 20 years, continuing in the style of his late friend, and his paintings were shown in many New York galleries.

. . .

The naturalist and artist Louis Agassiz was unsuccessfully working on the fossil of a prehistoric fish. He could only make out a vague outline until he dreamed 3 nights running what the fish looked like alive. The third night he left pen and paper by his bed and sketched the fish when he awoke from the dream. Carefully chipping away a last thin layer of rock, he revealed a new, undescribed fossil fish the exact image of the one he had seen in his dream.

. . .

When the playwright Ben Jonson visited a friend in Camden in 1603, he saw a vision of his eldest son, Benjamin, who was at that time in London. The boy appeared "with the mark of a bloody cross on his forehead, as if it had been cut with a sword." Jonson learned his son had died of the plague at the time of the vision.

. . .

Fra Filippo Lippi was a Carmelite monk. He was also one of the finest painters of the Renaissance. His model for his many portraits of the Virgin Mary was a beautiful nun. He left his order and ran off with her.

. . .

Alexandre Gustave Eiffel, designer and builder of the Eiffel Tower, incorporated into the design a love nest in which to carry on trysts high above the Paris skyline.

. . .

Auguste Rodin, the French sculptor, froze to death and the French government did nothing to save him. He was refused financial aid several times. In the winter of 1917, Rodin applied to live in a room in one of the museums that housed his sculptures. He was refused and a month later he died of exposure in a garret. His statues, meanwhile, had warm rooms to stay in, at government expense.

• • •

When the writer and naturalist Henry David Thoreau was on his deathbed, a relative asked him if he had made his peace with God. "I did not know we had quarreled," he replied.

THE MADNESS OF KINGS

When his mother learned Enrique Peñaranda had become President of Bolivia in 1940, Señora Peñaranda said, "Why, if I'd known Enrique would be president, I would have sent him to school." The dictator was illiterate.

A predecessor, Mariano Melgarejo, tied the British ambassador to a donkey and paraded him through the streets. When Queen Victoria was informed of the outrage, she ordered a map brought to her. With a flourish, she crossed off Bolivia. "Bolivia," she declared, "no longer exists."

• • •

Shamyl, a Caucasian bandit who waged Holy War against the Russians from 1834 to 1859, did not know what a million was. He captured the Czar's uncle and was offered a million rubles in ransom. Shamyl thought it was a trick and refused, saying he would not take one kopek less than 5000 rubles. He was paid.

• • •

Emperor Menelik II of Abyssinia became enamored of a recent invention, the electric chair, in 1890. He ordered three to be sent from the United States. They arrived and the emperor was informed they could not work—Abyssinia had no electricity. So Menelik used one for his throne.

• • •

During Benjamin Harrison's term of office (1889–1893), the White House was wired for electric light. President Harrison and his wife were said to be nervous about touching the light switches, for fear of being electrocuted, so they often went to sleep with all the lights blazing.

• • •

President John Quincy Adams had a pet alligator in the White House. The reptile was housed in the East Room, and the President got much amusement from watching guests flee in terror on encountering it.

• • •

U.S. president Franklin Delano Roosevelt became fed up with making small talk in receiving lines. He believed no one paid attention to the little pleasantries that were exchanged, so to prove his point he tried muttering as he shook each hand, "I murdered my grandmother this morning." Only one man was startled enough to reply, "She certainly had it coming!"

• • •

In 1862, the philanthropist Horace Norton was presented with a cigar by General Ulysses S. Grant. He saved it reverently as a memento and passed it to his son, who in turn passed it to his son, Winstead Norton. In 1932, Winstead delivered a speech at a reunion, and as a tribute to Grant, lit the cigar. It went BANG! After seventy years, Grant finally had his little joke.

•　•　•

Andrew Johnson, the 17th president of the United States, was illiterate when he married at age 18. His wife taught him to read and write. Johnson had been apprenticed to a tailor, and he made all his own clothes, and some of the First Lady's.

•　•　•

Abigail Adams, the second First Lady, hung her family's wash on clotheslines strung through the East Room of the White House.

•　•　•

Andrew Jackson married Rachel Donnelson before her divorce from her first husband was final. When he ran for President, the press hounded him, and he fought duels to defend her honor. One duel left a bullet in his lung, which became infected and had to be removed, without anaesthetic, when he was in the White House. Rachel died just before the election and Jackson remained bitter to the end of his days.

•　•　•

The first man appointed Secretary of Defense (the title previously had been Secretary of War) was James Forrestal. He was committed in 1949 to the mental ward of Walter Reed Army Hospital because he thought secret agents were following him. Secretary Forrestal killed himself by jumping out of a hospital window. As it turned out, his paranoia was justified. Israeli secret agents *had* been following him, to find out about the U.S.'s relations with the Arabs.

• • •

King George III of England went insane in his later years. During one of his attacks, he insisted on ending every sentence with the word "peacock." His ministers eventually cured him by telling him that "peacock" was a beautiful word but a royal one, which a king should only whisper to his subjects.

• • •

The omens were not favorable at the coronation of George III. The queen had a toothache, the Sword of State was mislaid, there were not enough chairs for all the nobility, and the high steward's horse, which had been trained to come in the hall and then back out, came in backwards. Worst of all, the largest diamond fell out of the crown. The Archbishop of Canterbury picked it up and said, "A jewel beyond compare will be lost to the Crown." The American Revolution was fought during King George's ill-fated reign.

• • •

Czar Nicholas II's reign began badly and ended worse. At his coronation in Moscow, gifts were given out to the people. But a rumor started that there were not enough to go around, and a stampede began. Hundreds of people were trampled to death. The czar's reign ended with the Russian Revolution, and he and his entire family were executed.

• • •

Perhaps the greatest stroke of genius of Russian Communist leader Nikolai Lenin was to name his party the "Bolshevik" party, which means "majority," even though it was a minority party. The name added prestige and eventually became a self-fulfilling prophecy.

• • •

When the Argentinian dictator Juan Perón was in exile in Madrid in 1971, he would dine nightly with his third wife, Isabel. The other dinner companion was always the corpse of his second wife, Evita, who had died 19 years before. Her body had been embalmed with glycerine.

• • •

Queen Marguerite of Navarre (1492–1549) wore a hoopskirt with thirty-four secret pockets, each enclosing the embalmed heart of a former lover.

• • •

Peter the Great of Russia (1672–1725) discovered his wife had a lover. He had the man beheaded and the head was pickled in a jar of alcohol. She was forced to keep it in her bedroom.

• • •

King Victor Emmanuel II of Italy (1820–1878) allowed his big toenails to grow for a whole year. On New Year's Day he would trim them and have the toenail clippings polished and bejeweled. Then he would present them to his favorite mistress of the moment. The mistress with the largest collection, Countess Mirafiori, eventually became the King's wife.

• • •

The Shah of Persia, on a state visit to England in 1889, failed to make a good impression when he tried to buy the Marchioness of Londonderry to be one of his wives. Later he told the Prince of Wales that if the ladies of the Prince's court were the Shah's wives, they should be beheaded to make room for prettier ones, because they were ugly.

• • •

Lady Cork (1746–1840) was a kleptomaniac. She could not be arrested or humiliated because of her station, so her lady's maid would go through her handbag and discreetly return items to various shops. Once she stole a pet hedgehog from a neighbor, but soon tired of it. She persuaded a baker to trade the hedgehog for a sponge cake. ''It will rid your bakery of beetles,'' she claimed. The baker had no beetles but knew better than to turn down a lady.

• • •

The Roman emperor Augustus (born Gaius Octavius in 63 B.C.) renamed the eighth month August in honor of himself. He then stole a day from February so that his month would have the same number of days as July, which was named for his uncle, Julius Caesar.

• • •

The Roman emperor Nero entered several events in the Olympic Games of 66 A.D. He was accompanied by 5000 bodyguards. The emperor was declared the winner of every contest, even if the other competitors had to fall down to let him win.

Nero's golden palace contained acres of orchards and a revolving dining room with a ceiling that sprinkled perfume. The roof was tiled with gold and the swimming pool inlaid with mother of pearl. When the emperor went swimming, young slave boys were instructed to pretend they were minnows and nibble on him.

Nero cherished a dream of being a singer. At one of his performances, he locked the doors so his audience could not leave. A woman gave birth in the stands. Three men escaped: one pretended to be dead and the other two carried him out.

• • •

King Alfonso of Spain kept a servant whose only job was to signal the King when the Spanish National Anthem was being played. The King was tone-deaf and relied on his man to tell him when to stand up.

• • •

It was a crime punishable by death for a commoner to touch Queen Sununda of Siam or her children. So when she and her two offspring fell into the Menam River when their boat sank in 1881, onlookers had no choice but to let them drown.

• • •

The oldest known printed book in the world was made 2195 years ago. It was found walled up in a cave on the Chinese border, and was probably hidden because the Emperor Ch'in Shi Huang-Ti (259–210 B.C.), for whom China is named, had all the historical books in his kingdom burned so that history would begin with him. He also built the Great Wall of China.

• • •

When Mao Zedong was Chairman of China in 1958, he started a campaign known as the Great Leap Forward, a disastrous attempt to modernize the country. All able-bodied men were ordered to set up and run backyard steel furnaces. Everything made of iron went into the primitive furnaces, down to cooking pots and pitchforks, only to emerge as useless, twisted lumps of metal, instead of the high-grade steel someone had told Mao would be produced. Worse, crops went untended because the farmers were at the furnaces, so there was a terrible famine.

Mao was a peasant and never brushed his teeth. He rinsed his mouth with tea in the mornings, then ate the leaves. His teeth turned green, then black, and fell out.

• • •

Czar Paul I of Russia became so incensed about jokes about his baldness that he decreed that anyone who mentioned the subject in his presence would be flogged to death.

• • •

Anne Boleyn, one of the six wives of Henry VIII, was executed, supposedly for being a witch. Among the "evidence" given against her at her trial was the fact that she had been born with six toes on one foot, six fingers on one hand, and three breasts.

• • •

When George Washington was elected president of the United States, there was a king in France, a czarina in Russia, an emperor in China, and a shogun in Japan. Only the office of president remains.

• • •

George Washington had to borrow money to go to his own inauguration.

• • •

After Thomas Jefferson was sworn in as president of the United States, he returned to his boarding house for dinner. Every seat was taken, and no man stood up to offer the new president a chair. After an uncomfortable silence, the wife of a senator from Kentucky offered her seat. A true Southern gentleman, Jefferson politely declined.

• • •

Thomas Jefferson introduced a bill in Congress that would have outlawed slavery in 1775, almost 100 years before the Civil War. It was defeated by a single vote. Jefferson's original draft of the

Declaration of Independence included a tirade against slavery, which he blamed on King George III. He was condemned for having "waged cruel war against human nature itself, violating its most sacred rights of life and liberty in the persons of a distant people. . . ." The references to slavery were deleted under protest.

•   •   •

Benjamin Franklin was not entrusted with the task of writing the Declaration of Independence because it was feared he would try to include a joke.

•   •   •

Abraham Lincoln and his cabinet raised a new flag over the White House on June 29, 1861, in honor of the new administration. As President Lincoln tugged the rope, the flag stuck, and when he pulled harder, the upper corner of the flag tore. Nine stars of the Union flag were torn from it.

•   •   •

Abraham Lincoln was so abused by his wife that his ambitions were probably furthered by his attempts to get away from her. Mary Todd Lincoln once hit him in the face with a piece of wood when he did not build a fire fast enough to suit her. She also pelted him with potatoes and books and threw coffee in his face. According to a recent biographer, Lincoln might have been content as a simple country lawyer if he had been more happily married.

•   •   •

Theodore Roosevelt was an ardent conservationist, and it went against his principles to cut down and display a live tree at Christmas. So he forbade the custom. There was such a public outcry, and his own children were so disappointed, that Roosevelt relented.

THE ABSURDITIES OF WAR

Hitler's mother seriously considered getting an abortion but was talked out of it by her doctor.

• • •

Minoru Genda, the Japanese officer who convinced his superiors of the feasibility of a surprise attack on Pearl Harbor, was awarded the U.S. Air Force Legion of Merit in 1959, when he was commander of the new Japanese air force.

• • •

In 1937, a Japanese commander named Kozo Nishino was taking on crude oil at a refinery near Santa Barbara, California. On the way to a formal ceremony welcoming him to California, Nishino slipped and fell into a patch of prickly pear cactus. Workers at the refinery had a good laugh at his expense. Apparently Nishino never forgot the incident, and in February 1942, he took his revenge by personally directing the shelling of the oil refinery from his submarine. One man was wounded and there was some minor damage.

• • •

War games in Louisiana in 1941 were brought to a standstill by 3 small boys with a toy cannon. Several thousand soldiers of the Blue army, on the banks of the Cane River were stymied when the three Prudhomme brothers, aged 14, 12, and 9, fired a loud popgun cannon at them. The soldiers fired blank machine guns and rifles. After a half hour of furious fire, an umpire signalled a ceasefire and asked Mrs. Prudhomme to tell her sons to stop shooting. "They are holding up the war and most of the Blue Army," he explained.

• • •

In 1889, a small fleet of German ships sailed into a Samoan harbor and shelled the island, destroying some U.S. property. American warships were immediately dispatched to counterattack, and they sailed into the same harbor. A hurricane hit Samoa and both fleets were sunk. Peace was declared as there was nothing to fight with.

• • •

Four newspapermen met in a hotel bar on a Saturday night in 1899. Desperate for a story for the Sunday edition, they concocted one stating that a group of American engineers were planning to tear down the Great Wall of China to symbolize international goodwill. The story was picked up as genuine by all the major newspapers in the U.S. and abroad. A group of Chinese patriots were inspired to riot in Peking, to kill missionaries, and to besiege foreign embassies. Twelve thousand troops from six countries were eventually sent in to put down what became known as the bloody Boxer Rebellion.

• • •

During the time Cuba was fighting for independence from Spain, the U.S. battleship *Maine* blew up in the harbor of Havana on February 15, 1898. Whipped-up anti-Spanish patriotism from the Hearst newspapers, who were locked in a fierce competition for readers, propelled the U.S. into the Spanish-American War over the incident. Careful tests proved in 1911 that the *Maine* had accidentally exploded from the inside and did not hit a Spanish mine.

• • •

The Spanish-American War was first declared by Spain against the United States. However, the United States backdated the declaration of war by 3 days, to look more heroic.

• • •

A bloody war was started over a postage stamp. The stamp was issued in Paraguay in 1932 showing a map of the Chaco region between Bolivia and Paraguay as belonging to Paraguay. It also said, "Has been, is, and will be." On June 15, Bolivia attacked to claim the Chaco area and by the time the war ended 3 years later, 100,000 men had been killed. The peace treaty awarded Paraguay about three-fourths of the disputed land.

• • •

Prussian statesman Otto von Bismarck tricked the French into declaring war against Prussia by changing the words of a telegram from the King of Prussia to the French. He made the conciliatory words of the king sound belligerent.

• • •

Alexander the Great was one of the best generals of all time. One story is a case in point. On his campaign to conquer India in 328

B.C., the king ordered his blacksmiths to make helmets, breastplates, and other armor many sizes larger than his men could wear. Alexander then left the oversize armor on the field, where the enemy would be sure to find it. The opposing force was terrified and demoralized at the prospect of fighting giants.

• • •

Allah-ud-din Khilji laid siege to Delhi in 1296. He ran out of ammunition for his catapults and started bombarding the city with 100-pound (45-kg) bags of gold. Delhi quickly surrendered.

• • •

In 1347 the Black Plague was raging through Europe. Citizens of Lübeck, Germany, tried desperately to appease the wrath of God by donating all their money and jewels to the monastery. The monks would not let the people in for fear of contamination, so the mob threw coins, gold, and jewelry over the walls. The monks threw it back. The back-and-forth of wealth continued for several hours, until the monks gave up and allowed it to pile up in their courtyard.

• • •

The walled city of Carcassonne, France, was saved by a pig, according to legend. The city was under siege by the Saracens and was in danger of being starved into submission. Dame Carcas hoarded all the grain she could find and used it to fatten her last pig. The lady then threw the pig over the wall, shouting defiantly. The Saracens believed that if the residents of Carcassonne had so much food that they could throw it away, their cause was hopeless. They folded their tents and went away.

• • •

Peking was defended against European invaders in 1860 by Chinese who waved paper tigers and dragons in a futile effort to scare them away.

• • •

The Sybarite people of ancient Italy taught their horses to dance to music. In 510 B.C. the Sybarite army attacked the city of Croton. The defenders struck up a lively tune, causing the horses to dance, and the Sybarites were slaughtered.

• • •

During the War of 1812, American naval officer Captain Oliver Hazard Perry feverishly constructed a fleet to take on the British on Lake Erie. The warships were bottled up on land for a full month as they were closely guarded by a British flotilla commanded by Robert Barclay. Barclay was ready to blow the Americans to smithereens if they tried to launch. But on July 30, 1813, Barclay sailed away. He was bored with the blockade and went to visit an attractive widow. He boasted to her the fleet would be stuck on a sandbar on his return. He was wrong.

Captain Perry, who popularized the slogans "Don't give up the ship" and "We have met the enemy and they are ours," was a young man of unquestioned courage. However, he had an irrational fear of cows, and would make large detours around fields if he so much as heard one mooing.

• • •

George Washington's small army camped at Valley Forge was freezing, starving, and demoralized in the terrible winter of 1777–1778. The British commander, General William Howe, might have easily overrun the encampment, but instead chose to spend the winter with a charming Philadelphia lady.

• • •

Tamerlane, who conquered most of Asia in the 1300s, was buried in a tomb in Samarkand, with an inscription that read, "If I am brought back to earth the greatest of all wars will engulf the land." The tomb was opened at 5 A.M. on June 22, 1941, at the exact moment Russia was invaded by the Germans, hundreds of miles away.

• • •

A soldier named Alex Ainscough of Cheshire, England, was stationed outside Rouen, France, in 1918. He walked into the strange town to get tobacco. He recalled: "I decided to investigate the street and the old turnings off it. It was a warm evening, and my decision had hardly passed through my brain when a strange chill struck me. I seemed suddenly to become familiar with my surroundings. I was marching with seven other men at the head of a column. We were all clad in black chainmail, and we were all tall. In front rode three men on horseback, also clad in black mail. We were going to see the burning of Joan of Arc. Here comes the strange part of my experience. I followed the street and eventually came to the outside of some kind of market, and on the pavement were marks cut into the stones. A tablet above stated that Joan of Arc had been burned on the spot."

• • •

During the First World War, a young Polish girl awaited the return of the soldier she loved. Merna began having dreams of him trapped in a dark tunnel. The recurring dreams became more detailed, and she saw images of a ruined castle on a hill, and heard Stanislaus crying for help. Months went by without word from him, so Merna set out to look.

She had no idea where the castle was, so she described it to everyone she met. She relied on strangers to feed her and she slept by the side of the road. On April 25, 1920, Merna came to the little village of Zloty, in southeastern Poland. There on the hill was the castle in her dream. She collapsed in the town square and a crowd gathered in curiosity.

When she revived she told them her lover was trapped in the ruins. The villagers were skeptical but, moved by her passion, began digging. After two days of work they broke through to a dark tunnel. A voice cried out and there was Stanislaus, thin and pale and blinking in the sunlight he had not seen in two years. An artillery shell had demolished the castle and trapped him in the rubble. He had lived on the castle's supply of cheese and wine with only rats for company. After a thorough investigation by the Polish Army, Stanislaus was given a discharge with honors. He married Merna, who had saved him through her faith in her dreams.

• • •

In the fierce battle of Bastogne, Belgium, in 1944, a soldier was knocked flat by an artillery shell. He was not wounded, but went blind. Doctors could find nothing wrong with his eyes, so he was hypnotized. He was made to relive the horror of the battle and his sight came back. The psychiatrist told him he had been wounded in the hand. When the soldier came out of his trance he complained of a burning pain in that hand, and it blistered and sloughed off, leaving a raw wound. The doctors were fascinated. They experimented on the hapless soldier and found they could produce cold sores and bleeding cuts on his fingers, and they could direct which would bleed and which would not, all by hypnotic suggestions.

• • •

Patricia Kord, a 28-year-old university secretary in Indianapolis, was undergoing hypnotic therapy for headaches in November 1957. She suddenly went into a very deep trance and spoke in a markedly different voice. The voice claimed to be that of Gene Donaldson, a young Confederate soldier. Richard Cook, the hypnotist, taped the procedure, and over the course of several sessions, the story of Gene Donaldson emerged.

He said he had been born and raised in Shreveport, Louisiana, and he described his neighbors, mentioning a Mr. Emmonds who ran the local bank. Donaldson described joining up with a group of young men heading off for war. His first battle was Shiloh, where he was blinded in one eye. With great hesitation he described being shot at the battle of Nashville, and dying during the night.

"Did it seem important to you—what they did with your body? Did you care?" he was asked by the hypnotist. "No, sir. You don't care where they put you!" he replied. He visited his mother but was unable to speak to her, and she could not see him.

Neither Patricia Kord nor Richard Cook had ever heard of the soldier Gene Donaldson, and neither had ever been to Shreveport. A search through Confederate Army records found a Private Gene Donaldson of Shreveport, Louisiana, had enlisted in the Louisiana Volunteers. They fought at Shiloh and Nashville; he was killed at Nashville. The names of the neighbors matched and there was a small bank owned by a Mr. Emmonds, which went out of business during the Civil War.

• • •

Colonel Thomas Berry was wounded in the battle of Chickamauga. The bullet lodged itself in his intestine and the doctor refused to operate, as such cases were considered hopeless. In desperation, Berry operated on himself. He had only a bullet to bite on for the pain and one nurse to assist. He found a "horrid fascination" in the procedure, as he opened the wound, found the hole in his bowel, removed the bullet, and cleaned and sutured the wound closed. Colonel Berry made a full recovery.

•   •   •

During World War II, a woman had a nightmare in which she saw her son sleeping in a tent with a tree about to crash down on him. She woke up terrified and called out his name over and over. At the same time, her son was asleep in a tent on an island in the Pacific. Troubled by a dream, he awoke and heard his mother calling. He stumbled outside. A palm tree fell, crushing the tent and the cot he had been asleep on, moments earlier.

•   •   •

During the battle of Agincourt in 1415, the French threatened the English archers that if they were victorious, they would cut off the first two fingers of the Englishmen's right hands, preventing them from ever firing another arrow. Henry V warned his bowmen of the threat. They won the battle and shot down knights in armor with their longbows. The English taunted the defeated French soldiers by showing them their first two fingers with palm reversed. This became the most insulting gesture an Englishman can make, to this day.

•   •   •

One of the earliest invented machine guns fired two kinds of bullets. Round bullets were for Christians, and square bullets, which did more damage, were for infidels.

•   •   •

Uriel Henkel of Parsons, Kansas, had part of his chin torn off by a bullet during the Civil War. He stuck the skin of a freshly killed chicken on the wound, and it took, later sprouting feathers.

• • •

John Russell Mackinson was a British soldier in the attack on Gallipoli in World War I. He was shot in the chest but not operated on, as the bullet was lodged in the heart and it was felt surgery would kill him. Mackinson returned home to Surrey, England, married, and ran a little hotel there for many years.

In the summer of 1936, Mackinson went on vacation and revisited the Turkish battlefield. Arm in arm with his wife, he strolled across it. Suddenly he yelled, "I say, Maggie, this is where the blighters got me!" and fell down dead. An autopsy revealed the bullet had suddenly shifted.

• • •

One day in 1893, Henry Ziegland abandoned his girlfriend. The brother of the girl shot Ziegland but only grazed him, and the bullet lodged itself in a tree in front of Ziegland's house. The brother, thinking himself avenged, killed himself with the same gun. Twenty years later, Henry Ziegland decided to remove the tree. His first attempts were unsuccessful, so he used dynamite. The explosion propelled the buried bullet into his head and killed him.

• • •

Daniel Spicer of Leyden, Massachusetts, was killed by two bullets on March 5, 1784. On January 25, 1787, his brother Jabez was killed during Shay's Rebellion, by two bullets. Jabez was wearing Daniel's coat, and the bullets passed through the same holes.

• • •

Ilija Sesum, a 90-year-old Yugoslav living in a village near Belgrade, coughed up a bullet he had been carrying in his body for 65 years. He was wounded in a battle on the Italo-Austrian frontier in 1916.

•   •   •

The Union charge was held up at Malvern Hill by a company of Confederates led by a brave young officer. The Union captain pointed him out to his best sharpshooter, a Sgt. Driscoll. Driscoll shot him, then turned over his body as they overran the position. It was his son. Driscoll was frantic in his grief and exposed himself to gunfire until he was killed later the same day.

•   •   •

General John Bell Hood and his division of Confederates marched through Chambersburg, Pennsylvania, on June 27, 1863. The ladies of the town jeered the soldiers and one lady stood defiantly in her doorway, draped with the Union flag. This prompted a Confederate to remark, "Take care, madam, for Hood's boys are great at storming breastworks when the Yankee colors is on them." She made a hasty retreat.

•   •   •

General Ulysses S. Grant was seen on only two occasions to lose his temper. Once he came across a straggler who was assaulting a woman. He leaped from his horse and hit the man with a musket, sending him sprawling. The other time, Grant saw a teamster hitting his horses in the face with a whip. Grant flew into a rage and ordered him tied to a tree for 6 hours as punishment.

He also never swore. He explained, "Well, somehow or other, I never learned to swear ... I have always noticed, too, that swearing helps to rouse a man's anger; and when a man flies into a passion, his adversary who keeps cool always get the better of him.''

• • •

The Plains Indians waged war in a civilized way. Warriors proved their bravery by "counting coup." Elaborate points were awarded for touching an enemy, hitting him with a coup stick, or, especially, for saving a friend's life. The least number of points were awarded for killing an enemy. Ceremonies took place after the battle, in which warriors recited their coup histories.

• • •

A tribe in New Guinea called the Tsenbaga have made warfare a protracted affair with little loss of life. A fight is postponed for several days until the battleground is cleared of underbrush. Then challenges, threats, and insults are exchanged. If this does not provide enough emotional release, two pigs are sacrificed and the warring parties sit down together and feast on the salty meat, which makes them sluggish. Once blows are exchanged, the battle is immediately halted if anyone is killed. More pigs are slaughtered and eaten, and the killer must perform rituals of atonement. Each truce gives both sides opportunities to resolve their differences without loss of honor.

Other tribesmen in New Guinea fashion elaborate headdresses of the feathers of birds of paradise when they prepare for battle. They make menacing noises and gestures with their spears, but if it starts to rain, everyone goes home so that the headdresses are not ruined.

• • •

The Toltecs of Mexico went to war with wooden swords to avoid killing anyone.

• • •

There is an unexploded nuclear bomb buried in a field somewhere near Goldsboro, North Carolina. In January 1961, a B-52 bomber fell apart in midair, releasing two 24-megaton bombs. One was recovered but the other sank in a waterlogged field and was lost.

• • •

Nikita S. Khrushchev, premier of the USSR from 1958 to 1964, went on a bender now and again with vodka. Once, in the midst of a drunken tantrum, he threatened to call the White House and "start World War III." Fortunately for all humanity, he passed out and was put to bed by an aide.

DANGEROUS DRESS

James Fotherington was the first man to wear a top hat on the streets of London. He caused such a commotion that he was arrested. Police charged him with having "appeared on a public highway wearing upon his head a tall structure of shining luster and calculated to disturb timid people." Fotherington had to pay the equivalent of $2,500 to be freed.

•   •   •

The philanthropist Jonas Hanway was jeered on the streets of London in 1750. His innovation? Carrying an umbrella. Umbrellas were only carried by women until that day.

•   •   •

The only woman ever to be awarded the Congressional Medal of Honor, Dr. Mary Edwards Walker, was honored for her medical service during the Civil War. Dr. Walker continued to wear men's clothing in civilian life, despite being arrested in New York City for "masquerading as a man."

• • •

Annette Kellerman, a swimming star from Australia, was arrested for ''indecent exposure'' on a beach in Boston. Her one-piece bathing suit ended in trousers 2 inches above the knee and exposed her elbows. The year was 1909.

• • •

In 1995, swimsuit fashions were made of incredibly impractical materials. There were suits made of cashmere, black velvet, flannel, fleece, and vinyl. Or how about swimsuits with metal zippers? Fine, if you don't want to get wet.

• • •

The first Englishman to wear suspenders, Lieutenant Andrew Bright of Nottingham, forgot he had them on when he undressed for bed. He tried to take his pants off with his jacket on, knocked over a candle in the struggle with himself, and burned to death.

• • •

Three teenage girls owned a kimono in succession, but all three died before they could wear it. A Japanese priest declared the kimono unlucky and ritually burned it in 1657. A freakish gust of wind caused the flames to spread. It quickly turned into the Great Fire of Tokyo, a holocaust that killed 100,000 people. Three-fourths of the city burned, including 500 palaces and 300 temples.

GOD IN COURT

A woman in Cherokee County, North Carolina, willed all her earthly possessions to God. The court went through the legal procedures in an effort to fulfill her last request and the sheriff's report reads: "After due and diligent search, God cannot be found in Cherokee County."

• • •

Mr. Ernest Digweed of Portsmouth, England, left his estate of $57,957 to "the Lord Jesus Christ" provided He shows up to claim it within 80 years. The interest on the invested money is to go to the Crown of England after 21 years. And if Christ fails to appear at the Second Coming, or if sufficient proof of His identity is not obtained by a public trustee, the Crown gets the whole pot.

• • •

When William Irvin III of Kansas City, Missouri, returned from the Gulf War, he fell on hard times. The Army veteran worked as an airport security officer, but was only making $12,000 a year, so he prayed for a windfall. The United States Government sent him a check for $836,939.13 by mistake. Irvin claims he thought it was a gift from God and cashed the check. He will probably end up in prison, possibly for as much as 43 years.

• • •

A New York state woman went to St. Jude's Church every day for nine days to pray to the patron saint of lost causes to help her keep her family together. On the ninth day, she thought her prayers were answered when she found an envelope stuffed with $10,000 at the foot of the shrine to St. Jude. Elated, the woman spent the money on an apartment and to send her daughter to beauty school. At the same time, an anonymous man called the church to say he had left a large donation in gratitude to St. Jude for helping him with his career. The parish priest brought charges against the woman for taking the money, which he felt belonged to the parish. The case was eventually dropped and the woman went free.

• • •

The Reverend Robert Wesley Hill landed in legal hot water because his congregation of 150 hearty souls praise God too loudly. The Minneapolis minister was jailed after neighbors of the True Apostolic Assembly Church lodged more than 70 complaints against the noisy church. Pollution control officers, sent to monitor noise levels during Sunday services, which feature amplified music, drums, and electric guitars, said decibel levels hit between 68 and 80, on a par with jackhammers or earth-moving machines.

• • •

Robert Schuller's Crystal Cathedral received complaints about its bells. The $5 million stainless steel carillon rings twice an hour, every day, between 9 A.M. and 6 P.M. A neighbor two doors down describes the bell-ringing as "the most gosh-awful noise you ever heard." What rankles even more is that the bells do not just play hymns. They ring a selection of tunes, including "Three Blind Mice" and "I Dream of Jeanie with the Light Brown Hair." Noise metres did not register levels of noise loud enough to qualify as a nuisance, however.

• • •

Three women from a Catholic church in Greensburg, Pennsylvania, became known as the "shouting ladies" after repeatedly disrupting services with their overly loud recitations of the rosary. The choir could not drown them out, even with microphones, and the priest said they frightened children. The women were jailed briefly and barred from the church.

• • •

The painter El Greco was brought before the Spanish Inquisition on the charge that he painted the wings of angels incorrectly. In those days a charge of heresy could lead to burning at the stake. El Greco was able to convince the inquisitors that he meant no offense, and he was acquitted.

• • •

An Italian motorist appeared in a German courtroom to explain why his car swerved off a road and crashed. The 51-year-old man explained he had taken his hands off the wheel and asked, "God, can you drive?" The man's lawyer noted, "The good Lord failed His driving test." In May 1994, a panel of judges found the Italian guilty of dangerous driving, recommended him for psychiatric treatment, and suspended his license for 20 months.

• • •

A lawsuit filed in Little Rock, Arkansas, in 1987 tried to forbid schools from celebrating Halloween as it is an "observation of the rites of Satan." The suit was filed on behalf of Jesus Christ and the children of the area.

• • •

When Richard Slyhoff died in 1867, he left instructions to be buried under a leaning rock in Jefferson County, Pennsylvania. He felt that on Judgment Day, when the earth trembled, the rock would fall and hide him from the Devil. But over the years, erosion and the forces of nature have moved the rock 10 feet (3 metres) away from his grave.

FREAKISH DEATHS

Thorton Jones awoke to find that he had cut his own throat. After gesturing urgently to his wife for pen and paper, he wrote: "I dreamt that I had done it. I awoke to find it true." He died a short while later.

• • •

Robert Ledru, a well-known French detective, was recovering from overwork at the French resort of Le Havre. His chief asked him to investigate the mysterious death of a vacationing businessman who had been shot at night on a beach near the detective's hotel. The clues were: a bullet from a Luger and the footprints of the murderer, which showed that he had been wearing socks and was missing a toe. Ledru's foot was missing the same toe and the socks he slept in had been wet. His Luger had been fired. After test-firing his own gun and comparing the bullets with those of the killer, Ledru turned himself in for the murder, which he apparently had committed in his sleep.

• • •

The coroner in a case in Butler County, Pennsylvania, said Michael Ricksgers claimed he "heard the bang and heard her moaning, and he woke up and he had a gun in his hand." Ricksgers killed his wife with a bullet to the heart, using the gun she slept with to protect herself, but claimed he did it in his sleep. The jury rejected his story.

• • •

Esther Winkelman was a world traveller of status that few attain. The retired doctor had visited 304 countries, islands, and territories, and had long since qualified for membership in the Traveler's Century Club, an organization open to visitors of 100 or more countries. When Winkelman reached her eighties, friends urged her that so much travel was dangerous. Her standard reply was that the trip to the airport was the most dangerous part of any journey.

On January 17, 1993, the 86-year-old Winkelman was being driven to the Kansas City International Airport for the first leg of a trip to the remote island of Tristan de Cunha. Her friend's car was in an accident, and Esther Winkelman, globetrotter, died in her hometown hospital.

• • •

Duke Antonio Ferdinando never took a drink in his life, because he had been warned by a soothsayer that alcohol would kill him. On April 19, 1729, he returned from a hunting trip, soothed his aching muscles with rubbing alcohol, caught fire, and burned to death.

• • •

A young woman in Miami falsely believed she had cancer, so she drank herself to death—with water. She drank as much as 4 gallons a day, in an attempt to flush her body clean of disease. The Dade County medical examiner explained that the excessive water intake had destroyed her body's chemical balance.

• • •

Three people were asphyxiated by carbon monoxide fumes during a Navaho healing ritual. A cedar fire built inside a mud-and-wood hut called a hogan produced the deadly gas. The hogan was built with modern building materials, which sealed in the smoke. Older buildings have gaps in the walls.

• • •

An apartment dweller in Gweru, Zimbabwe, got behind in his bills. A municipal worker was sent to cut off the electricity, but he accidentally clipped the wrong wire and electrified the water pipes. The man took a shower and was electrocuted.

• • •

A bolt of lightning hit the railing of the eighth floor of a building in Brooklyn, knocking loose a flower pot. The flower pot hit a 28-year-old woman walking down the street below and killed her.

• • •

A lawyer was representing clients accused of recklessness in a fatal boat accident on a lake in Shreveport, Louisiana. The lawyer took a boat out on the same lake, stood up during a thunderstorm, raised his hands in the air and yelled, "Here I am!" A lightning bolt struck him dead.

• • •

Bobby Leach survived a brutal ride in a barrel over Niagara Falls that broke multiple bones in his body. On a lecture tour in New Zealand, however, he slipped on a banana peel and was killed.

• • •

A woman in Saint Austell, Cornwall, was taking clothes off the line in her garden. A 5-foot (1.5 m) hole opened under her feet and she fell in and was killed. Investigators thought it might have been an old well or mineshaft.

• • •

With more than 30 years' experience, a matador who had killed more than 2000 bulls in his career was knocked down on a ranch in Madrid and killed when a yearling bull charged him from behind.

• • •

A hunter named Ali tried to pin the head of a snake to the ground with the butt of his shotgun. The snake thrashed to get free, wrapped its tail around the gun, looped its tail through the trigger and pulled it.

• • •

A man in Thailand ate four bags of locusts as a tasty snack. He succumbed to insecticide poisoning.

• • •

While breaking into a villa in Enna, Sicily, a burglar raided the refrigerator, then collapsed. The owner had prepared food and laced it with rat poison. The burglar's partner surrendered to police after calling an ambulance.

• • •

Henri Villette of Alençon, France, took his cat to the river to drown it. In the act of throwing the cat in the water, Villette lost his balance. He fell in the river and drowned. The cat swam ashore.

PEOPLE ARE STRONGER THAN YOU THINK

When explorer David Livingstone was mauled by a lion in Africa he described his reaction: "The shock produced a stupor similar to that which seems to be felt by a mouse after the first shake of the cat. It caused a sort of dreaminess in which there was no sense of pain nor feeling nor terror, though [I was] quite conscious of all that was happening." When the lion let go for a moment, Livingstone recovered and got away. This reaction, which has been described by others in life-threatening situations, appears to be the body's merciful defense against pain in hopeless situations.

• • •

In November 1972, Bob Hale jumped from his plane and discovered that neither his regular nor his backup parachute would open. He fell 3,300 feet at a rate of 80 miles an hour and landed on his face. He later said, "I know I was dead and that my life was ended just then. There was nothing I could do." A few minutes after hitting the ground he stood up and walked away with nothing worse than a broken nose and a few missing teeth.

• • •

Mark Mongillo took his 12th skydiving jump on June 19, 1977, in Florida. At 2,500 feet (760 m) he pulled the ripcord, but his body was not arched, so he fell headfirst and the parachute wrapped around his body. He pulled the reserve, but it too became entangled and wrapped him like a cocoon. He said out loud, "Shoot, I'm dead, God help me." Then he watched the ground approach over his shoulder. It took about 30 seconds for him to drop and a lot went through his mind. "I just thought I was dead; I accepted it; I didn't panic or anything; I wasn't scared."

He remembered thinking, "At least I'm not going to feel any pain when I hit the ground; it'll be quick." Mongillo was relaxed when he landed and he didn't even get knocked out. He landed on his back, bounced twice and heard his leg break. He also bruised his kidneys badly, and a rib punctured his liver, but he eventually went back to work. He had fallen half a mile and was moving at about 120 miles (192 km) per hour when he hit the ground.

• • •

An 18-year-old girl name Kimberly Lotti was returning home from work in her pickup truck in Quincy, Massachusetts. The truck smashed through a chain link fence. A pole 2 inches in diameter flew through the windshield and impaled her. It passed through her upper chest and extended 5 inches (13 cm). "It was eerie," she recalled, "I didn't feel any pain at all. I thought the pipe was just pressing against my arm." The pipe missed all her vital organs and was safely removed.

• • •

Nicholas Alkemade bailed out of a burning plane at 18,000 feet without a parachute. He remembered looking at his feet and seeing stars, and realizing he was falling head first. He landed in a fir forest and slid down a snow bank, both of which broke the fall. The only injuries he received were those he suffered in the plane, 3½ miles (5.6 km) up.

• • •

A ball turret gunner, Alan E. Magee, was trapped when his B-17 was hit over St. Nazaire, on January 3, 1943. At 22,000 feet (6600 metres) he managed to escape through a hatch, but had no parachute. Two French children witnessed his body cartwheeling down, lit up against the night sky by fires on the ground. Magee landed on the glass roof of the St. Nazaire railroad station at the exact instant a bomb went off inside. *The glass did not break, and Magee was not killed.* The two events cancelled each other out. A German rescue team brought him down and he spent 3 months in the hospital, making a full recovery.

• • •

The Reverend Johannes Osiander (1657–1724) of Tübingen, Germany, led a remarkably charmed life. During his career he was charged and knocked down by a wild boar, but was uninjured; his horse fell on him, trapping him without injuries; he escaped a fusillade of gunfire from bandits; he was buried in an avalanche but dug himself free; he was blown into the Rhine River by a blizzard, but climbed out unaided; he had a tree fall on him with enormous impact, but was unscathed; and he survived a shipwreck only to be accidentally plowed under by the ship intent on his rescue. True to form, he popped to the surface unharmed. What finally did him in is unrecorded.

• • •

Steven Newman accomplished what few other persons in history have done. He walked around the world. Newman survived charging wild boars, runaway horses, and almost being eaten by ants. Secret police in Turkey kicked him awake and interrogated him, but he escaped through a window. Bandits with machetes nearly killed him in Thailand, pickpockets thrashed him in Morocco, and a drunken thief almost shot him in Australia. Yet he dwelt on the positive encounters, saying, "It was the acts of love from the people I had met—and the people who cheered me on—that have enriched my life beyond description." Newman walked 21,000 miles in four years, returning to his home town of Bethel, Ohio, on April 1, 1987.

• • •

During the fourth race at Bay Meadows Racetrack in San Mateo, California, on May 8, 1936, a horse stumbled. That started a chain reaction that sent jockey Ralph Neves crashing to the ground. His horse, Flanakins, landed squarely on top of him. Three doctors at the scene declared Neves dead. The 18-year-old jockey was taken to a cold storage room at a morgue, stripped to his pants and one boot, and wrapped in a sheet. Half an hour later, a doctor friend looked in at his body. On impulse, he felt for a pulse and found one. The doctor gave Neves a shot of adrenaline, and the jockey woke up with a start and ran out of the morgue.

He ran two miles (3.2 metres), then hailed a taxi to the racetrack. There was a sensation when he was recognized. The same doctors who had found him lifeless, with no heartbeat or respiration, looked him over and found nothing worse than mild shock and some bruises. Ralph Neves raced the next day and that same year he won the title for having ridden the most winners at Bay Meadows Racetrack. He retired 28 years later and is in the Racing Hall of Fame.

• • •

A shepherd named Mutata became a legend in Kenya in the 1970s. When he was just 3 years old, he apparently died and was being buried when he cried out and was rescued. At age 19, he vanished. After 6 days his body was found in a field. Mututa was being buried again when he opened his own casket. In May 1985, a surgeon declared him dead. He lay in state for a day, then woke up and asked for water. In September of the same year, he died again. His brother laid his body out for two days just in case. This was the last time. After the first three experiences, Mutata said he visited heaven, where the angels told him it was a mistake and sent him back.

• • •

Poon Lim had shipped as a second steward aboard the *Benlomond*, which was torpedoed on November 10, 1942. The ship sank near the Equator, in the South Atlantic, 750 miles east of the mouth of the Amazon River. He saw five other survivors taken prisoner by the U-boat that sank them; then he was left alone in a limitless sea. Poon Lim found a life raft with food and water for 50 days. After a week, a ship sighted the raft and approached for a look, then steamed away without him as if they feared a trick. That was his bleakest moment. Poon Lim summoned his inner reserve and drew on the example of his mother in Hong Kong: her strength, energy, and resourcefulness. He trapped rainwater with a canvas awning and fished with a spring from a flashlight. The fish were too small to sustain him, so he extracted a nail from the raft with his teeth, causing excruciating pain, but he made a fishhook large enough.

After 100 days, airplanes spotted him from the air and dropped dye markers. A sudden storm dispersed the dye, contaminated his precious water supply, and swept away his food. He drifted for 5 days under the broiling sun, drinking his own urine until his body could produce no more, too dehydrated to even weep. A bird landed on the raft and Poon Lim devoured it.

After 133 days, a world record which Poon Lim hoped would never be broken, a Brazilian fisherman rescued him. He was strong enough to walk ashore unaided. After his story came out, he was given many awards, including one from the English government: "To Poon Lim, bravest of the brave."

• • •

During a bad winter storm in the Midwest on January 19, 1985, two-year-old Michael Troche woke up in the early morning and wandered outside, dressed only in light pajamas. His parents were fast asleep and he wasn't found for several hours. It was a killing −60°F (−45.5°C) and little Michael froze. Ice had formed on and beneath the skin, he was rigid and stiff, and his body was heard to crack when it was moved. He had stopped breathing. At the hospital his core temperature measured a record low 16°F (−8.9°C). Yet he was revived and brought back from the brink of death with no brain damage. He had been "flash frozen" by the icy wind, and that and his youth had probably saved his life.

• • •

Kazumi Kimata of Japan had his arm amputated below the elbow in an accident with heavy machinery. His doctors told him they couldn't reattach it. So Kimata took the arm home, put it in a plastic bag, prayed over it, and buried it in his garden. Six hours later, a doctor offered to try the surgery. So the 31-year-old man dug up his arm and took it to the hospital. Kazumi Kimata's arm is now working fine.

• • •

A 34-year-old Yugoslav bus driver named Hamdija Osman was repairing the bus's brakes at the edge of a cliff. The bus started to roll toward the 400-foot (120 metre) drop and Osman jammed his left leg under the wheel. The wheel rolled over his leg, breaking it in four places, and the bus continued toward the cliff. Osman jammed his *other* leg under the wheel and stopped the bus, saving the lives of thirty passengers.

• • •

Matthew Williams, an 18-month-old child, was knocked down and run over by a car in Worcestershire, England. A tire rolled right over the baby's stomach but, remarkably, he was unhurt.

• • •

A Frenchwoman who sold pencils to Vincent van Gogh was asked to what she attributed her longevity, after she celebrated her 120th birthday. "God must have forgotten me," she replied.

• • •

Researchers descended on the tiny town of Campodimele ("field of honey"), Italy, to find out why residents live such long lives. A higher proportion than normal are between 75 and 99 years old, and most of them enjoy a healthy active life in extreme old age. A simple, healthy diet and lots of exercise seems to be the answer, but resident Pasquale Pannozzi, 83, had a different reason. "This is a perfect spot. No stress. Who would want to die?" he asked.

• • •

Professor Albert von St. Gallen Heim fell 66 feet off a cliff in Switzerland. "...I saw my whole past life take place in many images, as though on a stage at some distance from me.... Everything was transfigured as though by a heavenly light and everything was beautiful without grief, without anxiety and without pain.... Like magnificent music a divine calm swept through my soul," he recalled in 1892. He was not badly injured.

INDEX